Contents

CW00385205

Published by
The Bible Reading Fellowship
15 The Chambers
Abingdon, OX14 3FE
United Kingdom
Tel: +44 (0)1865 319700
Email: enquiries@brf.org.uk
Website: www.brf.org.uk
BRF is a Registered Charity

ISBN 978 0 85746 402 6
First published 2016
10 9 8 7 6 5 4 3 2 1 0
All rights reserved

Acknowledgements
Scripture quotations taken from The Holy Bible, New International Version Copyright
(Anglicised edition) copyright © 1973, 1978, 1984, 2011 by Biblica. Used by permission
of Hodder & Stoughton Publishers, an Hachette UK company. All rights reserved. 'NIV'
is a registered trade mark of Biblica (formerly International Bible Society). UK trademark
number 1448790.

Scripture quotations taken from The Holy Bible, New International Version, copyright ©
1973, 1978, 1984, 1995 by International Bible Society, are used by permission of Hodder
& Stoughton, a member of the Hachette Livre UK Group. All rights reserved. 'NIV' is a
registered trademark of International Bible Society. UK trademark number 1448790

Scripture quotations taken from The New Revised Standard Version of the Bible, Anglicised
Edition, copyright © 1989, 1995 by the Division of Christian Education of the National
Council of the Churches of Christ in the USA, and are used by permission. All rights
reserved.

Scripture quotations from THE MESSAGE. Copyright © by Eugene H. Peterson 1993, 1994,
1995. Used by permission of NavPress Publishing Group.

Scripture quotations from the Good News Bible published by The Bible Societies/
HarperCollins Publishers Ltd, UK © American Bible Society 1966, 1971, 1976, 1992, used
with permission.

Scripture quotations from The Living Bible copyright © 1971 by Tyndale House Foundation.
Used by permission of Tyndale House Publishers Inc., Carol Stream, Illinois 60188. All
rights reserved.

Extract from As a Child by Phil Steer, published by lulu.com, 2012

Cover photograph: © Thinkstock

Every effort has been made to trace and contact copyright owners for material used in
this resource. We apologise for any inadvertent omissions or errors, and would ask those
concerned to contact us so that full acknowledgement can be made in the future.

A catalogue record for this book is available from the British Library

Printed by Gutenberg Press, Tarxien, Malta

The Editor writes...

One way of viewing prayer is through intercession—asking God for things, joining in with him in the work he is undertaking on earth.

Prayer is also about praising God, recognising him for who he is and thanking him for what he has done, for individuals and for humankind.

Our aim may be that every action, thought, moment is lived with and for God. This appeals to those of us who have never been good at half measures! Part of this is learning to make the most of the moments that occur when time could be spent facing God. One of my favourite times in the summer is sitting on the bench in my garden in the evening. I listen to the birds, enjoy the flowers and the warmth of the sun, finding God in all those things he has given me, and in the stillness that descends on the garden in the late evening as everyone goes inside and settles for the night. It is a time beyond words, when, as someone once said, 'I look at him and he looks at me' and we know we love each other. Try it one evening, or some other quiet moment. If you find it difficult to settle, don't give up, stay with it for a few minutes more. It sometimes takes a disciplined approach to overcome the cacophony inside us.

Sometimes it is in remembering to look for God as I go about the simple daily tasks. Is he there as I switch on my computer, put the washing on the line, walk to the shops, weed the garden, wash the car? What do I know of God from his accompanying me during those times?

As you work through this issue of *Quiet Spaces*, my prayer for you is that you find your own special moments and places of prayer, of encountering God, and that you will be open to finding him there, maybe in some unexpected places and at unexpected times. After all, we know a God of surprises. Prepare to be surprised.

Sally Smith

Writers in this issue

Ann Persson is a Trustee of BRF. She enjoys using her love of nature and of God's word in the Quiet Days she leads. She is author of *The Circle of Love: Praying with Rublev's icon of the Trinity* (BRF, 2010) and *Time for Reflection: Meditations to use through the year* (BRF, 2011).

Sally Smith enjoys creating spaces that enable encounters with God through leading Quiet Days and creating prayer corners and stations. She has led prayer groups in her local church, works as a spiritual director and writes and produces education materials.

Claire Musters is a freelance writer and editor, mother of two, pastor's wife and school governor. Claire's desire is to help others draw closer to God through her writing, which focuses on marriage, parenting, worship and issues facing women today. To find out more visit www.clairemusters.com and @CMusters on Twitter.

Amy Boucher Pye is a writer, speaker and editor. An American married to an English vicar, she's the author of *Finding Myself in Britain: Our Search for Faith, Home & True Identity* (Authentic, 2015). She loves running the *Woman Alive* book club, writing Bible reading notes and speaking to varied groups.

John Fitzmaurice is Director of Ordinands and Vocation in the Diocese of Worcester. He has a master's degree in the psychology of religion and a doctorate in ecclesiology, as well as a deep ongoing interest in monastic and apophatic spirituality.

Lisa Cherrett is BRF's Project Editor and Managing Editor for Bible reading notes. She sings, writes haiku poetry and is interested in the relationship between Christianity and contemporary culture. She blogs at lisannie44.wordpress.com.

Andrea Skevington lives in Suffolk with her family. She writes for both adults and children, recently winning the Christian Book of the Year award (Speaking Volumes) for her retelling, *The Lion Classic Bible* (Lion Hudson, 2011). She also enjoys storytelling for children and running creative writing seminars for adults.

Jean Sims offers spiritual accompaniment and enjoys leading quiet days, providing prayer spaces and guiding retreatants. She belongs to the prayer and spirituality group in her diocese and helps to lead courses on prayer and in the training of spiritual directors for the Diocese of Southwell and Nottingham.

Pamela Evans enjoys leading Quiet Days, speaking, and seeing men and women become more fully the people God created them to be. Her books include *Shaping the Heart* (BRF, 2011). Having recently moved to Hampshire, Pamela is enjoying exploring the area and seeing more of her grandchildren.

Mountain encounters

Ann Persson

Mountains

Introduction

There is something mystical and majestic about mountains. Although the result of violent activity, either volcanic or the upthrust caused by the movements of tectonic plates, they do represent permanence and stability. Their beauty is captured in many a photograph and painting. For some, mountains are irresistible invitations to climb, to hike in or to enjoy the thrill of winter sports. For others, they are hideaways and places of refuge. About ten per cent of the world's population live on the slopes or foothills of mountains.

Those who have ever climbed a mountain will remember the elation of reaching the summit and then that sense of awe. There is a greater sense of perspective from that height and a feeling of being 'removed from' or separated from what is below. No wonder so many encounters with God in the Bible took place on mountains.

Mountains are mentioned over 500 times in the Bible. They dot the landscape of biblical regions; they litter the psalms; are the scenes of battles and, most importantly, are places where God chooses to reveal himself and communicate to his people.

Recall your own experience of being at the top of a hill or a mountain. How did you arrive there—on foot, by car, train, cable car or ski lift? What were the views like and how did it make you feel being there? Did you find your thoughts turning to God? Imagine yourself back there. Invite God to sit with you and listen to his description of what he sees. You might want to look for some pictures of mountains to accompany you as you explore this theme.

Mount Moriah

Imaginative

God had asked big things of Abraham, one of which was to leave his home in the city of Ur in Mesopotamia and journey to Haran in Canaan. God had also made a huge promise to him, that he would be the father of a nation which would be as numerous as the stars. Abraham and Sarah had no family, but amazingly, in their old age, their treasured son Isaac was born. Now Abraham, whose name means 'father of many', was being asked the biggest thing of all—to sacrifice his only son, now an adolescent, on a mount in the land of Moriah. It didn't make sense for his son to die when Abraham had been promised numerous descendants, and it would break his heart and Sarah's. Nonetheless he set out with two trusty servants and Isaac to journey to Mount Moriah. This was possibly the hardest journey of his life. The final climb to the mountain that God had indicated must have been horrendous, especially when Isaac asked his father where the lamb for the sacrifice was.

Read the story in Genesis 22:1–19 and then imagine you are Abraham. You may find it helps to write it down as the story unfolds, or just enter the events and become part of them.

Imagine yourself as Abraham leaving Sarah, camping out under the stars at night and remembering God's promise. Notice the first sighting of the Moriah mountain range, imagine having to tell Isaac the truth. Notice how it feels as you tie your son and place him on the unlit fire. How do you respond to God when you see the ram and offer him instead as a sacrifice?

Mount Sinai

Reflective

Moses was asked by God to lead his people out of slavery in Egypt and journeyed with them for 40 years towards the promised land. God had dramatically made their escape possible but now the people, about 600,000 of them, were facing the challenges of nomadic life in the desert, and grumbling and tensions broke out. God needed to act to give them some structure to hold them together. He summoned Moses and Aaron to climb Mount Sinai so that he could speak to them there. Picture the scene: the people gathered expectantly, trumpets sounding loudly, the sky grows dark and there is thunder and lightning; from the top of the mountain billows thick smoke and the mountain shakes. It is in this setting that God speaks and delivers his ten commandments. Read them in Exodus 20:2–17.

The first four concern our relationship with God and the remaining six govern our human relationships. God's laws are timeless and they challenge us. They need to be the scaffolding in the building of our lives.

Jesus was asked which commandment was the most important. He replied, 'Love the Lord your God with all your heart and with all your soul and with all your mind. This is the first and greatest commandment. And the second is like it: "Love your neighbour as yourself"' (Matthew 22:37–39, NIV). Spend some time with these two commandments. What do they mean for you? How do you follow them daily?

Same mountain, different person

Going out/prayer

Read 1 Kings 19:1–18.

Elijah was one of God's boldest prophets. His name means 'My God is Yah(weh)' and, true to his name, he stood up for God in a time when idolatry swept his land. The prophets of Baal (supported by the powerful Queen Jezebel) and of the false god Asherah were defeated on Mount Carmel (18:16–40).

Jezebel was furious at the loss of her prophets, and swore to kill Elijah. Afraid, he ran to the wilderness, sat under a broom tree and, in his despair, asked God to take his life. Instead, the prophet slept, and an angel brought him food. Strengthened, Elijah walked on for 40 days to Mount Horeb (an alternative name for Mount Sinai). He climbed up the mountain, found a cave, crawled into it and spent the night there.

God questions him, 'What are you doing here, Elijah?' meaning, 'Why have you come here?' His answer would suggest that he is still afraid for his life and has come to hide, which, of course, God knew all the time but wanted Elijah to acknowledge.

God tells him to come out of his cave, stand on the mountain in God's presence and then watch, listen and feel, to experience God's promise. A violent wind blew up and it was hard to keep his balance but he did not sense God in it. Next an earthquake shook him and the mountain cracked but God was not in it. Fire broke out and he feared for his life but there was no God to draw near to him. He retreated into the cave but then came a gentle whisper, maybe calling his name and once more the question came, 'What are you doing here, Elijah?' and he replies with the same answer as before, but now comes a directive from God, 'Go back the way you came.' Face your demons and take action as I will direct you.

'Be still, and know that I am God' (Psalm 46:10) or, as the Good News Version puts it, 'Stop fighting, and know that I am God.' It is often our own inner noise, disturbance and fire that prevent us from hearing God, who speaks so gently and with such economy.

Spend some time being still before the God who meets us not in the earthquake or the wind, but with a gentle whisper in a cave. If you live near a cave, you might visit and in the silence and darkness wait with God, or find a quiet hiding place, and allow your inner noise to quieten, then listen for the quiet voice of heaven.

> *And his that gentle voice we hear,*
> *Soft as the breath of even,*
> *That checks each fault, that calms each fear,*
> *And speaks of Heaven.*
> HARRIET AUBER (1773–1862)

Mount Zion

Prayer

Mount Zion is commonly understood as the temple mountain in Jerusalem. King David with his small army captured Jerusalem from the Jebusites and ordered the ark of the covenant to be brought there. His son Solomon had the magnificent temple built, which was described as the earthly dwelling place of God. It became the focal point for Jewish celebrations, and pilgrims (including Jesus) came to worship in the temple. It is the pivotal mountain between the Old and New Testaments.

The temple mount was considered to be holy ground but anywhere is holy ground, for God is everywhere, around us and within us. We need only to open ourselves to him. The apostle

Paul wrote, 'Don't you know that you are God's temple and that God's Spirit dwells in you?' (1 Corinthians 3:16, NRSV).

Use this action prayer to offer your body as God's temple.

Touch your eyes

God bless my eyes so that I may see you clearly in what you have made.

Touch your ears

God bless my ears so that I may hear what people say to me but also hear the words I speak to others.

Touch your mouth

God bless my mouth so that I may speak with truth and understanding and that I may speak up for those whose voice is not heard.

Touch your head

God bless my thinking that it may spring from a place of inner peace.

Touch your heart

God bless my heart and fill it with your love and compassion.

Touch your hands

God bless my hands that they may show care and generosity.

Touch your feet

God bless my feet so that I may walk in your ways through life.

Mount of temptation

Prayer

Read Matthew 4:1–11.

The time came for Jesus to leave home and to head for the river Jordan where his cousin John is baptising. He asks to be baptised and as he comes up out of the water hears the voice of his Father, 'This is my Son, whom I love; with him I am well pleased' (3:17, NIV). He will hear the same words on a mountain three years later.

The crowd around is open and eager to hear him. Surely it is a good place to start his ministry—but no, he feels compelled by the Spirit to leave the Jordan and travel towards the Judean desert. Sand, shingle, twisted shapes of limestone, intense heat by day and cold by night; sleeping under the stars and waking each morning to the colours of sunrise. This was a barren place of solitude without any distractions, and he spent 40 days there.

For Jesus it is a place of testing. The Spirit intends that Jesus will emerge from the test with clarity of vision and clear goals, equipped and empowered for the challenges ahead. Satan has other plans.

Eventually, Satan takes Jesus to the top of a high mountain so he can see all the kingdoms of the world and their splendour. 'All this I will give you if you will bow down and worship me,' says Satan. Acknowledge that Satan is the prince of this world and he will stop competing with Jesus and give him all he wants. Simple. Jesus counters with strong words 'Away from me, Satan! For it is written "Worship the Lord your God, and serve him only"' (4:10). And the devil left him—for a season.

Have you ever thought that Jesus must have told his disciples of his experiences—laying bare his heart and soul but also letting them know that he has been tempted and tested? Really tested, he is able to help those of us who experience times of testing.

Find a photograph taken from the top of a mountain. See the extent of the lands you can see. Imagine being offered all this. Take some time to talk with Jesus about the testing and the temptations that you face. He understands and will give you the strength to counter them again and again if necessary.

Places of prayer

Going out/reflective

Throughout his three years of ministry, it was to the mountains and the hills around Galilee that Jesus withdrew when he wanted to spend time with his Father. When he needed to choose twelve men to be his close disciples, Jesus spent the night in prayer on a mountainside. It was an important decision. He would pass on to them the teaching about the kingdom of God; after his death they would take the gospel to different parts of the earth and would set up the church in his name. When morning came, he walked down and chose twelve men to be his apostles (see Luke 6:12–16).

We are told in Luke 5:15–16 '… crowds of people came to hear him and to be healed of their illnesses. But Jesus often withdrew to lonely places and prayed.' After busy days he would spend time in the evening or through the night climbing up until he found a sheltered place on the mountain. Wrapping his cloak around him, he would sit under the stars, quiet and alone save for his Father's presence.

Go outside and find a quiet place to sit. You may have a mountain or hill nearby that you can visit, or you may have another favourite place to go to. As you set off, invite God to journey with you, notice his presence as you travel. When you arrive, sit down with God and begin telling him about your life at the moment, pouring out your heart to your heavenly Father. Tell him about any decisions you may be facing and seek his advice.

The Sermon on the Mount

Imaginative

Read Matthew 5:3–15 and 6:5, 14.

Wherever a crowd gathers, Jesus of Nazareth is usually at the centre of it. He has created such a stir around the towns and villages of Galilee with his fresh teaching and his healings.

Imagine the scene: a hill above the lake, where all is quiet and still. What can you see? What can you hear?

Become aware of Jesus approaching with a crowd of people behind him. Listen and watch as they arrive and chat. Talk to those around you to find out who they think he is.

The crowd settles in a grassy area that is like a huge amphitheatre. Jesus sits down and a hush falls on the crowd as he begins to teach. He looks around at everyone gathered there, men, women, children, and you. With great compassion, he begins telling you all that you are blessed if you are humble, sorrowful, gentle, justice seekers, merciful, pure, peacemakers, even if you are persecuted for the cause of right. This is not the kind of teaching you are used to. How does the crowd react? How do you react?

He goes on to say that you are like salt of the earth and the light of the world, but you must not lose your saltiness nor hide your light. These are things you understand. He is speaking directly to the people.

Then he speaks about prayer and slowly he prays a prayer to

his heavenly Father, who is also our Father in heaven. It is a holy moment. You know the prayer well, but hear it as if for the first time. Join with Jesus as he prays to his heavenly Father.

Gradually the crowd disperses and you are left alone with Jesus. Sit with him and talk about what you have just heard. Let him speak to you about it and how it plays out in your life.

Mount of Transfiguration

Reflecting

The compassionate work of Jesus was focused on people disfigured by diseases or evil spirits. He transfigures them by God's power at work in him, changing them by raising to life, restoring, healing, forgiving, setting free.

The day comes when Jesus is transfigured by the Father who loves him. With three of his closest disciples, Peter, James and John, he climbs a mountain to find a place where he might spend time in prayer. It is not named in scripture but is most likely to have been Mount Tabor in Galilee. The net is tightening and the religious authorities are out to get him. He needs to be sure of the path that God the Father is taking him on, not to cancel out his mission but to fulfil it. As he is praying, something happens to him. His face becomes radiant and he starts to glow. Beside him appear Moses and Elijah representing the law and the prophets. They talk with Jesus about his impending death and then they are enveloped in cloud. Moses and Elijah have disappeared but from the cloud comes the Father's unmistakable voice, 'This is my Son, whom I love; with him I am well pleased. Listen to him!' (Matthew 17:5). Almost the same words that were spoken over him at his baptism.

After the mountain-top experience, they descend to the base only to find a young boy seized by convulsions and in need of healing and deliverance. The work of transfiguring the disfigured goes on.

Recall a mountain top experience you have had. Return to it in your memory. Notice God present with you and what it was that was so memorable. Then fast-forward to see how it impacted on your life in the following days and months. Where was God after you came down from the mountain? How has he continued to be with you in that experience since?

Mount of Olives and the hill of Calvary

Reflecting

It is the last week of Jesus' life on earth and he fulfils scripture by riding into Jerusalem on a donkey, allowing the crowds to hail him as the Messiah. At the Passover meal, Jesus takes a cup of wine and declares, 'This is my blood of the new covenant, which is poured out for many for the forgiveness of sins' (Matthew 26:28). He walks out through the city gates, down the hill, across the Kidron Valley and up to the Garden of Gethsemane on the Mount of Olives, a favourite place of his for withdrawing. Here, among the olives, he kneels in prayer, asking his disciples to stay awake.

He cries out, 'My Father, if it is possible, may this cup be taken from me' (26:39). He contemplates what it would mean to drink the cup of sacrifice. He could have avoided it. He could have run away into the desert and founded a community; he could have made a surprise attack on the city; many would take up arms for him, but he chose to stay in Gethsemane knowing the consequences and he ended his prayer with 'Yet not as I will, but as you will.'

Arrest followed quickly; a night of beatings and endless questioning, until morning came and the sentence to death by crucifixion was pronounced. Then a slow, painful trudge to Mount Golgotha and the agonising experience of being nailed to his cross, which was then jolted into the socket. For six hours Jesus hung between life and death in excruciating pain. At last came his faint words, 'Father, into your hands I commit my spirit' (Luke 23:46). And with that he died. Such love! Redeeming love for the whole world for all time—redeeming love for you and for me.

Spend some time before Christ on the cross on Mount Golgotha.

> When I survey the wondrous cross
> On which the Prince of glory died,
> My richest gain I count but loss,
> And pour contempt on all my pride.
> See from His head, His hands, His feet,
> Sorrow and love flow mingled down!
> Did e'er such love and sorrow meet,
> Or thorns compose so rich a crown?
> Were the whole realm of nature mine,
> That were an offering far too small;
> Love so amazing, so divine,
> Demands my soul, my life, my all.
>
> ISAAC WATTS (1674–1748)

The mount of the great commission

Creative

Read Matthew 28:16–20.

Three days after his death, as he had predicted, Jesus gloriously rose from the dead. The tomb was empty and Jesus, mistaken for the gardener, appeared to Mary Magdalene on that first Easter morning. He entrusted her to take the message of his resurrection to his 'brothers', the disciples, at a time when a woman's word counted for nothing in a court of justice.

Many days later he instructed his disciples to go to a mountain, possibly the mount where he had delivered his great sermon, and he would meet them. It was here that he commissioned them to go and make disciples of all nations, baptising them in the name of the Father and of the Son and of the Holy Spirit (the first time the three names are used together) and to teach the people to obey everything that Jesus had commanded them. Then came the great promise, 'And surely I am with you always, to the very end of the age' (v. 20).

His work on earth was accomplished and handed on to men and women who would act and speak in the power of the Holy Spirit.

What is Jesus asking you to do?

Make a list of the main things you do for Jesus. Talk to him about them. How does this fit with the great commission of the disciples? Are there changes Jesus is asking you to make?

A Jesus encounter

Imagination

This is an exercise that will stretch your imagination but if possible, go with it. It can yield fresh understanding of yourself and your relationship with Jesus Christ.

Find a quiet, comfortable place.

Jesus has arranged to meet you at a favourite place of yours where you can be completely alone. It's up to you to choose the place. Let a place come to mind, maybe somewhere on a mountain. Imagine setting out to make the journey to the place you have chosen.

As you draw near to the spot, you realise that Jesus is already there. He is waiting for you. What feelings arise in you as you walk towards him?

As you come close, he is standing before you. He is looking at you. What does the look in his eyes say to you? What is your reaction to his presence?

He speaks your name and tells you how glad he is that you have come. How do you respond?

He asks what it is about this place that is special to you.

He invites you to sit down and to talk about your friendship. He begins by telling you why he enjoys being with you. And you listen.

You tell him what your friendship with him means to you and the effect it has had on your life. And he listens.

He responds and then asks if there is any concern that you have that you want to share with him.

You listen to what he has to say about it.

Jesus speaks again, 'Do you have a question that you would like to ask me?' You take your time to reply or simply stay silent.

He then asks you some questions. You do not reply to them immediately, in case you blurt out the expected answer. Rather, you let them echo and re-echo in your mind, observing how your heart reacts to them, until you can answer truthfully.

Again using your name, he asks,

'… who do you say that I am?'

'… what do you want?'

'… do you truly love me?'

After listening attentively, he turns to look fully at you and says, 'We are together in everything—you in me and me in you; you working with me and me working with you. Though you cannot see me, my Spirit is always with you.'

What does it feel like to hear those words of Jesus?

The time has come for him to go, so together you look ahead.

What kind of future do you want your relationship to have?

In what ways can you develop your side of it?

Your personal encounter has come to an end. You bring your conversation to a close and say 'goodbye' to each other.

His presence fades away and you are left to savour the mood that meeting Jesus has produced in you.

It was your mountain encounter.

Women Jesus met

Sally Smith

Jesus and women

Reflective

Stop and think for a moment. Who do you think of when you think of the women Jesus met? Who comes to mind? Are there any common characteristics?

As we explore the place of these women who came near to Jesus, spend some time remembering that they were women, and question how they represent the women Jesus meets today. What do you bring to Jesus as the man or woman that you are? Does your gender affect the person you are before God?

These women are real people experiencing life in all its variety. They are rich and poor, with and without children or husbands. They are loving and angry, struggling and passionate. They come to Jesus with their own needs and with those of others. They look for Jesus and they are found by him.

Having met Jesus, the response of many of these women is to serve him. This is often in domestic ways, but there are many other ways in which we can serve Jesus, as Jesus says, 'Truly I tell you, just as you did it to one of the least of these who are members of my family, you did it to me' (Matthew 25:40, NRSV).

Both men and women can learn from these women. We can learn what it meant to be a woman and how Jesus treated women. We may also learn how we can treat individuals and value them for their individual and generalised characters.

Ask God to enable you to be open to learn from them and to be touched by the strength of their stories as you journey with them and with Jesus.

Salome

Visual

Read Matthew 20:20–24.

Salome was one of the women who looked after Jesus during his time of ministry. They provided for him from their personal resources. Salome was also the mother of the sons of Zebedee, mother of James and John.

As Jesus talks about the coming kingdom and his coming death, Salome asks if her sons could sit on his right and his left in that kingdom. She doesn't just drop it into the conversation; she brings her sons to Jesus and kneels before Jesus to ask the question. I wonder what James and John were thinking and feeling. They must have been in agreement to some degree, as when Jesus asks them if they can drink from his cup, they reply yes they could; they are in fact eager to follow Jesus and to be those closest to him. This is a deliberate, serious act that Salome undertakes for her children. Jesus asks what she wants as she kneels before him. Her reply is her genuine request at that moment. We can argue about her motivation and her desire to see her sons doing well and in a place of standing and merit, but her heart is asking for what she believes to be the best for her sons.

Who are the people you would go on your knees before God for? Who would you ask for great things for?

Jesus' response to Salome is that he cannot grant her request. It isn't in his power to do so; those places have already been allocated. He tells the rest of the disciples (who are probably angry because they hadn't thought of asking for this first) that it is not great to be the ruler, that those who are first will be last, they will be the slaves, and that if they want to be great they will need to be servants. He reminds them that he came not to be served but to serve.

Think about the ways in which you serve others. It may be in practical things like cleaning or gardening, or it may be by listening or encouraging. Find objects that represent your service to others (a duster, or a mug for the tea you drink as you listen). Thank God for the skills he has given you to enable you to serve in these ways. Hold before him the people you serve. Then, when you are ready, place the objects before God. This could be in your prayer place if you use one or before a cross. Offer these acts of service to God—not that he may exalt you, but that he may be in what you do and that you may be serving him in your actions.

The poor widow

Imaginative

Read Mark 12:41–44.

This is the well-known story of the poor widow who gives two small copper coins to the treasury in the temple.

Imagine if it happened in your church. As you see the scene unfold, notice what is happening inside you. How do you respond to the actions you see? What are you thinking as you see the individuals make their gifts? It's the point in the service where money is collected. Obviously wealthy people (how do you know they are wealthy?) put their cheques or wodges of notes on to the plate. A poor widow (how do you know she is a poor widow?) puts a couple of coins on the plate.

Hear Jesus' words when he saw this happening in the temple, 'Truly I tell you, this poor widow has put in more than all of those who are contributing to the treasury. For all of them have contributed out of their abundance; but she out of her poverty has put in everything she had, all she had to live on' (v. 44).

Recall how you were feeling and what you were thinking. Don't be critical or proud of yourself; just notice your reaction and be honest with what happened.

Admit before God how you reacted. Offer to him your reaction. Thank him for all those who contribute financially to the work of your church, and remember those who do it unseen as well as those you see.

Woman with a haemorrhage

Imaginative

Read Mark 5:25–34.

Have you spent time in a crowd? It may have been a sporting event, or it may have been in a queue or at a concert or festival. As you spend time within the crowd, you start to notice some of the people. You may begin to talk to them, or you may just watch them and begin to build up the story of their lives in your head.

In this passage we have a crowd who had spent time waiting for Jesus to come across the water and then following him. They would have got to know each other as they jostled along together.

Imagine being in that crowd. Notice the people around you, the families, groups of friends, people on their own. They are from different walks of life, some known to each other before, some complete strangers. Walk with them as you follow Jesus. Be aware of him walking within the crowd, of people trying to get near to hear him or ask him questions. Notice how you get knocked and bumped into.

Begin to notice some of the people around you.

You particularly notice one woman who is on her own. She looks ill and poor. She seems anxious to get closer to Jesus. Do you just watch or do you talk to her?

She makes it to within touching distance of Jesus, and you see her reach out and touch his cloak.

Jesus quickly turns round and asks. 'Who touched my clothes?'

Feel the crowd around you and wonder how he knew the woman had touched his cloak.

Hear the disciples say, 'You see the crowd pressing in on you; how can you say, "Who touched me?"'

Watch as Jesus continues to look around at the crowd.

The woman comes, frightened, to Jesus and falls at his feet and starts to tell him what she has done and what has happened to her. You hear the details you could only imagine before, how she had been bleeding for twelve years and had spent all her money on physicians she hoped could cure her, but she had only become worse. How she knew that Jesus would be able to make her well if she could just touch him, and so she had reached out to him. And you hear her say that her haemorrhaging stopped and she felt in her body that she was healed.

Jesus listens to the woman and then says, 'Daughter, your faith has made you well; go in peace, and be healed of your disease.'

Watch as she leaves Jesus. What can you tell from how she walks about what she is feeling?

Jesus turns and looks at you. What would you want from him if you were able to touch his cloak?

He comes near and invites you to reach out and to touch his clothing. Dare you do it? Do you tell him what you want? Spend some time close to Jesus and listen as he responds to your story.

Hear as he says, 'Daughter/Son your faith has made you well; go in peace, and be made whole.'

Leave Jesus and make your way out of the crowd, holding close what Jesus has done for you.

Jairus' daughter

Imaginative

Read Mark 5:22–24 and 35–43.

The healing of the woman with a haemorrhage happens in the midst of another encounter, this time with a young girl. Her father is a leader in the synagogue, and when his daughter is seriously ill, he begs Jesus to visit and make her well.

So, imagine the crowd waiting by the sea for Jesus to cross over. Notice the people around you. See the people waiting for Jesus. Listen to their conversations.

Then Jesus appears. One of the leaders of the synagogue sees Jesus, rushes up to him and falls at his feet. He is begging Jesus, 'My little daughter is at the point of death. Come and lay your hands on her, so that she may be made well and live.'

Watch as Jesus listens and then joins Jairus and heads off.

You get separated from Jesus and by the time you catch up again, things have changed. You see them standing and some servants have arrived from Jairus' house. You overhear them say, 'Your daughter is dead. Why trouble the teacher any longer?'

Jesus also overhears and says, 'Do not fear, only believe.' And he indicates that Peter, James and John are to follow him and Jairus back to Jairus' house. Listen to the comments of those around you before you hurry off to follow Jesus.

When you arrive at the house, there is a crowd causing a commotion outside. Hear their weeping and loud wailing. Then push past and into the house where Jesus says, 'Why do you make a commotion and weep? The child is not dead but sleeping.'

How do you react when you hear these words? Those around you laugh at the words.

Everyone is sent out of the house except the girl's father and mother and those who had followed Jesus to the house. You follow them to where the girl is lying. See her, aged about twelve, lying still. Watch her parents as they enter the room.

Jesus takes the girl's hand and says to her, 'Little girl, get up!' and she gets up.

Watch those in the room. How do you feel? What are you thinking?

Jesus tells everyone to keep what has happened a secret and tells them to get her something to eat. Then he comes over to you. What do you want to say to him? What do you want to ask him?

Spend as long as you need to with Jesus, either talking or just being together.

Simon Peter's mother-in-law

Creative

Read Matthew 8:14–15.

This is a simple story of healing—Simon Peter's mother-in-law has a fever. Jesus enters the house and touches her hand, the fever goes, and she gets up and starts to serve him. She is able to serve because she has been healed.

When has Jesus touched you? If you keep a journal, you could look back and be reminded of how you have been touched in the past. What did you do after receiving from Jesus in this way? What is your response to the gifts of God?

Peter's mother-in-law immediately served Jesus. This would have been in a practical way, providing him with food and drink. There are many ways in which we can give back after we have received from God. At another point Jesus says, '… give and it will be given to you. A good measure, pressed down, shaken together, running over, will be put into your lap; for the measure you give will be the measure you get back' (Luke 6:38, NRSV) .

Proverbs 11:25 says, 'A generous person will prosper; whoever refreshes others will be refreshed' (NIV).

What have you been able to do because of what God has done for you?

You could write a letter of thanks to God for the gifts he has given you that have enabled you to serve him in different ways. Remember to focus on what you have been able to do because of what he has done for you.

Woman of Samaria—living water

Going out

Read John 4:7–15.

This is perhaps the longest conversation we have a record of between Jesus and a woman. She is a woman who in that culture Jesus should not have been speaking to anyway. As a holy man he should not have allowed himself to be alone with a woman, and if that did happen, he should not have entered into a conversation with her—there was thought to be a risk of impurity and gossip. Historically the Jews and the Samaritans had nothing to do with each other; they certainly wouldn't share eating and drinking vessels. This woman was of dubious character—she was visiting the well when it was likely to be quiet so that she wouldn't meet anyone there.

Yet Jesus does spend time with the woman and shows that he knows who and what she is. He offers her 'living' water, another way of describing what we call running water. This water he was offering was fresh water with no danger of it being stagnant. It would be refreshing water that would invigorate the person who drank it.

Either go out to a fast-running stream or waterfall, or run the tap.

Listen to the water. Watch it and enjoy the way the light reflects and moves.

Put your hands under the water. Feel it refreshing you. Wash your hands and face in the water.

Jesus said to the woman, 'Everyone who drinks of this water will be thirsty again, but those who drink of the water that I will give them will never be thirsty. The water that I will give will become in them a spring of water gushing up to eternal life' (vv. 13–14).

As you enjoy the fresh water before you, receive also the living water Jesus was offering the woman. Let it touch, not just your mouth and throat, but all parts of your life. Imagine it reaching into the hidden places and the unloved places, the places in need of cleansing and in need of watering and bringing back to life. Thank God for his generous gift.

Every time you turn on the tap or drink water over the next few days, remember the living water Jesus offers and thank him again for his gift.

Woman of Samaria—I know you

Reflection

Read John 4:16–26.

After offering the woman living water, Jesus shows that he knows all about her. He knows the details of her past she might prefer to keep secret, the events that have made her a woman to be avoided. In John 1 Jesus has shown that he knew

Nathaniel through and through. Both Nathaniel and the woman have immediately recognised Jesus for who he is. The woman's response is not to hide from Jesus or to run from someone who knows her in such detail. Her response is to go and tell the people of the city that she has met someone who has told her everything she has done. For her the good news that Jesus brought was that he knew everything she had done and still offered her living water. As a result of this, Jesus and the disciples stayed an extra two days in this city in Samaria.

What does Jesus say to you that makes you want to tell others about what he has said? How would you sum up why you follow Jesus? This may be different from why you started following him, and may not be what you expect, so allow some time and space to tell Jesus why you follow him.

You might like to write in your journal an explanation that you could give to someone of why you follow Jesus.

Martha

Creative

Read Luke 10:38–42 and John 11:20–27.

We all think of Martha as the one who was busy in the kitchen and who got cross because her sister didn't help with any of the jobs. She's the one to whom Jesus said, 'Martha, Martha, you are worried and distracted by many things; there is need of only one thing. Mary has chosen the better part, which will not be taken away from her' (Luke 10:41–42).

But it was also Martha who ran out to meet Jesus after the death of their brother, Lazarus, and who had the conversation with Jesus about resurrection and it was Martha who recognised Jesus as the Messiah (John 11:23–27). She obviously had a good relationship with him as she was able to trust and believe him and to recognise who he was. It is unlikely that she changed drastically, and so this closeness would have grown from her activity and busyness around Jesus. She would have chatted to him as she worked, and I can imagine him sitting watching her and chatting to her as she cooked.

Spend some time being busy with Jesus. As you go about some of your daily tasks, imagine Jesus sitting and watching you. Chatter away to him as you work and allow him some space to talk to you. Use the time to get to know each other better and to come closer to him. Does this make a difference to how you perform your tasks, or to your perception of them?

Mary

Imagination

Read Luke 10:38–42.

Mary is described as sitting at Jesus' feet and listening to what he was saying. Later in John's Gospel she anoints Jesus' feet with costly perfume (John 12:1–8), but let's stay with Mary at the feet of Jesus, listening to his teaching. We don't know what he was teaching, but here we're going to use the beatitudes from a few chapters earlier on in Luke's Gospel.

If you can, sit on the floor beside a chair. Imagine Jesus in the chair and just sit at his feet, being in his presence and listening to what he has to say to you. If sitting on the floor is not possible, imagine sitting beside Jesus.

You could read the Beatitudes (Luke 6:20–26) and listen to Jesus teaching you. What does he draw out as important for you personally?

How does it feel to be this close to Jesus?

Are you aware of Martha busy in the background or are you focused on Jesus and what he is saying?

The Syrophoenician woman

Intercession

Read Matthew 15:21–28.

This passage has the power to shock us. Jesus refuses to listen to the Canaanite woman because she isn't a Jew. She recognises him as the Son of David, but he doesn't answer her as she pleads for him to rid her daughter of a demon. His ministry is to the people of Israel and he is focused on that goal. But she isn't put off. She keeps shouting after Jesus and his disciples. Eventually, he responds and she kneels before him, pleading for him to help with her daughter. After their discussion, Jesus recognises the faith that has brought her to him and he allows himself to be distracted from his main ministry and to drive the demon out.

How persistent can you be when addressing Jesus? Do you have the woman's drive to keep asking the one person who can help?

Take a situation you have been praying about for a long time and hold it again before Jesus. If you need to, follow the woman's example and shout at God. Be prepared to argue your case and to keep going.

Jesus tells a parable about a woman who was persistent in prayer (Luke 18:1–8). She kept asking until the judge gave in. God will give justice to his chosen ones.

Women before the cross

Reflective

Read Mark 15:40–41.

Gathered around the cross we have several of the women who had followed Jesus and whom we meet briefly at different points in the Gospels. They have provided for him and are to play a significant role in the days after Jesus' death. They are joined by many other women who had come with Jesus from Jerusalem.

A suitable place to end this section would be to join these women around the cross in the last hours of Jesus' life.

Find a crucifix, or a picture of Jesus on the cross.

Look at the cross and Jesus on it. Respond in whatever is appropriate for you at his point.

What do you want to say to the women who are gathered around the cross?

What does Jesus want to say to them, and to you?

Friendship

Claire Musters

You are my friends

Introduction

The word 'friendship' probably conjures up very vivid pictures in your mind. You may have close friends whom you've known since childhood and with whom you've shared many great moments over the decades. There may be others you have recently met, but who nevertheless enrich your life. You may also think of friendships that you have lost through the passage of time or that have painful memories attached to them.

Jesus gathered a group of friends around him. They were his disciples, and at times they let him down, but nevertheless he also called them friends. John 15 shows us what his definition of friendship was: 'You are my friends if you do what I command' (v. 14, NIV). The previous verses reveal that his command was for them to love one another as he had loved them. This chapter is an amazing picture of how we are grafted into friendship with God, and of Jesus' part in that.

In this section we are going to focus on the concept of true friendship, on what being a friend of God means and how each of us can be a good friend to others as we learn more about friendship with him.

What does friendship mean to you?

Creative/visual

What does the word friendship mean to you? You could create a word map/collage of all the qualities you feel a friend should have. Alternatively, put together a pin board or scrapbook with photographs of friends, some of the places you've visited, activities you've done together, photos of gifts they have given you, and so on.

Take a little break from what you have created and then, when you come back to it, reflect on what jumps out at you. Is there a particular element that you find striking? Think about the reasons behind why you picked that; what does it reveal to you about friendship?

If you feel able, write a short poem based on what you have created. Then pray, thanking God for friendship.

True friendship

Reflection

John 15:13 says, 'Greater love has no one than this: to lay down one's life for one's friends.' This is an incredibly challenging verse. Friends are such a blessing to us, and yet how many of us would be willing to die for them? That is what Jesus says friends who truly love one another would do. Is this how we see friends? I view as friends those who do me good; who look out for me, cherish me, make me feel good about myself. Yet what do I consciously do for them to help their lives be better? Can I describe myself as Proverbs 18:24 does: 'There is a friend who sticks closer than a brother'?

What if, in this digital age, we have lost the art of true

friendship to a degree? For example, are 'friends' on social media real or simply 'trophies' we collect to make ourselves feel more popular? There are many good things about Facebook—I have reconnected with friends that I shared primary school with in the States. While I enjoy those interactions, what I treasure most about my close friends is the way we 'do life' together. This can be in a practical way if I'm ill and struggling to look after my kids and they offer to look after them. Friends also sense when I am feeling low and send me a verse that encourages me or they offer to pop by and pray. But they also have the guts to challenge me when my behaviour is not as it should be. While I may find that hard I am more than grateful that they do it. As God 'disciplines the ones he loves' (Hebrews 12:6) we need those in our lives who will speak the truth in love (see Ephesians 4:15). I hope I am faithful in doing these things for them too.

Take some time to consider prayerfully whether you are a true friend to those around you, and the ways in which you can grow as a friend.

Abraham: a friend of God

Spotlight

It would help if you could familiarise yourself with Abraham's story in Genesis 12, 15, 18, 20 and 22.

God conversed directly with various characters in the Old Testament but only Abraham was given the title 'friend of God' (see 2 Chronicles 20:7; Isaiah 41:8; James 2:23).

In Genesis 18 we have an interesting insight into God and Abraham's relationship. As his friend, God entrusted Abraham with a secret: he let Abraham know what his plans were for the wicked city of Sodom. Why did God let Abraham intercede for a city that he knew couldn't be saved? Through it, Abraham began to work with God, and learn about his supremacy, justice, mercy and love. Leadership qualities were being formed within Abraham.

Abraham was willing to sacrifice all for God (Genesis 22). In an act that provides a foretaste of the sacrifice Jesus would make for us, God asked Abraham to sacrifice his son. This seems offensive to us but God was testing Abraham's heart. He was also revealing how hard it is to give up something so precious—a son—and yet that was precisely what God would do for us.

God may give us a gift or talent that he then asks us to give back to him, in order to see whether we have somehow elevated that gift above him. When Abraham passed the test, God provided a substitute for Isaac—a ram caught in thicket. A sacrifice was necessary and, again, this reveals God's heart for friendship.

How can we be friends of God?

Reflection

Abraham was called 'friend of God'. God also conversed with Moses face to face, spoke to Elijah and did amazing miracles through him. And that's just what's in the Old Testament—what about the close friendships Jesus had with his disciples and the amazing way that God revealed the books of the Bible to the writers (such as John's incredible vision for Revelation)? Do we dare to think we could ever be so close to God?

The cross is the ultimate symbol of friendship. It was the way that God reconciled us to himself, and now the invitation is open for us to be intimate friends with him. Who are we to question whether we are holy or humble enough, when God himself has invited us?

So, how do we grow closer in our friendship with God?

One of the things that God has been saying to me in recent months is that he wants me to go deeper. For many years I have longed to have the same deep passion and desire for him that others I read about have, and I can be frustrated when I don't feel it. I do have a sense of him beckoning me closer and that he wants me to do more seeking. We live in an instant society, where information is at the tip of our fingers and we are encouraged to buy what we want *now*. God is saying we need to take time to seek him. As Jeremiah 29:13 says, 'You will seek me and find me when you seek me with all your heart.' I think we need to be more proactive, patient and wholehearted in our search for closeness with God.

One of the ways we can cultivate that sense of longing is by spending time within the psalms, soaking in the language that others have used to describe their own desire to be close to God. Take Psalm 63:1: 'You, God, are my God, earnestly I seek you; I thirst for you, my whole being longs for you, in a dry and parched land where there is no water.'

Linger over this verse, using all your senses to appreciate fully what the writer is saying.

As John 15 says, we are also to remain, or 'abide' in him (v. 5, NRSV). In the psalms David says, 'Lord, who may dwell in your sacred tent? Who may live on your holy mountain? The one whose way of life is blameless, who does what is righteous, who speaks the truth from their heart' (Psalm 15:1–2, NIV).

Wow, that is a very exacting standard! Thank God that he provided a blameless sacrifice on our behalf so that we *can* dwell with him.

'The Lord confides in those who fear him; he makes his covenant known to them' (Psalm 25:14). The Living Bible puts it like this: 'Friendship with God is reserved for those who reverence him. With them alone he shares the secrets of his promises.'

An old hymn says:

Trust and obey, for there's no other way
To be happy in Jesus, but to trust and obey.
JOHN H. SAMMIS (1846–1919)

Often we have the choice of whether to trust that God is our friend when circumstances try to prove otherwise. Brother Lawrence, a 17th-century monk, learned the art of 'practising the presence of God'—dwelling with him whether at prayer or working in the kitchen. If you find it hard to involve God in your daily activities, why not try setting an alarm every half hour, and then pause to reconnect with God and ask him to come and be a part of whatever you are doing next.

Jesus calls you friend

Meditation

Read John 13.
  Jesus knew that the time for his sacrifice was approaching. He was about to share his last meal with his disciples; he used that time to reveal how much he loved them, as well as what was going to happen.
  Imagine you are in that upper room with Jesus. Make yourself comfortable, get into a relaxed position, maybe close your eyes as you consider the following questions.

What does the room look like? Does it feel like just another evening relaxing with Jesus or is the atmosphere charged? Do you feel something is going to happen?
What is the food like?
How do you respond when Jesus suddenly gets down from

the table, wraps a towel around his waist and begins to wash people's feet? Do you feel, like Peter, that he shouldn't be doing something so lowly?

How do you feel when he talks about being betrayed? Confused? Hurt?

Jesus begins to explain that he has to leave you, to go to prepare somewhere for you. What is your response?

Do you believe him when he says you will do even greater things than the amazing miracles you have seen him do?

Your head is already spinning with all the mysterious things Jesus has said, but now he adds, 'I no longer call you servants, because a servant does not know his master's business. Instead, I have called you friends, for everything that I learned from my Father I have made known to you' (John 15:15, NIV).

How is your heart responding? Jesus is telling you to love those around you, that he is going to be leaving you soon, that you will be hated by the world. It all seems too difficult to understand, too negative to accept and yet…

Something in your heart is singing because *he called you friend*.

When you are ready, quietly finish your reflection and then spend some time worshipping God out of the thankfulness bubbling up in your heart.

Walk

Going out

Take a walk in a local park or town centre. Notice the different groupings of people—friends come in all shapes and sizes. You may want to sit in a café and 'people watch'. Ask God to open your spiritual eyes truly to understand the richness of friendships.

What is it that you see friends doing that speaks to your heart? Perhaps one friend helps another by holding her baby while she buys her coffee, or another carries some bags for his friend. Perhaps you'll spot someone sharing and then crying and see his friend comfort him. Consider what it is that you find such a blessing when you meet a friend yourself. Is it simply their company, the chance to chat and pray together, their practical help or a shoulder to cry on when necessary?

You could end this time by having a drink and chat with God in a café or by meeting one of your friends there to talk through what insights you've discovered—and to enjoy their company.

Friends aren't perfect

Bible reading

Read Matthew 20:20–28 and Matthew 26:36–46.

The Gospels describe how the disciples were with Jesus throughout his ministry. We've also seen and meditated on the fact that Jesus called them friends. But they weren't perfect. They let him down badly many times.

In Matthew 20 we see James and John with their mother, approaching Jesus to see if he would allow them to sit on either side of him in heaven. The other disciples get annoyed about their request—not because it was a terrible thing to ask, but because they all secretly wanted that privilege! Jesus saw their hearts and used it as an opportunity to teach them about how important serving one another is and that that was his ultimate purpose in coming (see vv. 26–28).

Turning to Matthew 26, we see Jesus in anguish. He asks his most trusted friends to stay close by while he prays. However, they fall asleep and each time he returns to them, he finds them sleeping. How this must have increased his sense of loneliness—

such a simple thing he asked of them and yet they let him down in his time of need!

We can all remember times when our friends disappointed us. Think about what your response was. Did you choose to forgive or were you harsh, determined to make them know how badly they made you feel? How do you think God is asking you to respond to those who hurt you?

… one another's

Bible reading/response

There are many 'one another' verses in the Bible, which highlights the importance God places on us being good friends to those around us. Some of them are given below. Spend some time reading the verses and make a note of any that really challenge you. Come back to them regularly over the next week, asking God if you need to make any changes in your life as a result.

'Love one another…' (John 13:34–35; Romans 13:8; 1 Peter 3:8; 1 John 3:11, 23; 4:11–12; 2 John 5). As you can see from the long list of scriptures, this is the command given most often. We've been reflecting on what loving one another means. How could you show your friends today that you love them?

'Serve one another humbly in love' (Galatians 5:13). How can you serve your friends best? Do you know what their pressing needs are?

'Be devoted to one another in love. Honour one another above yourselves' (Romans 12:10). This is about 'preferring' others over yourself. It can be quite a difficult discipline to master as our society wires us for selfishness! Philippians 2:3 also says, 'In humility value others above yourselves'. What are the ways in which you can do this?

'Be patient, bearing with one another in love' (Ephesians 4:2). How often are you impatient with your friends? How can you cultivate this vital gift of the Spirit more fully?

'Spur one another on towards love and good deeds' (Hebrews 10:24). We need those in our lives who encourage us to be the best we can be, and we need to do the same for our friends. In 1 Thessalonians we are urged to 'encourage one other' (4:18 and 5:11). One of the great ways to do this is through accountability or mentoring partnerships, where you get together regularly, pray for one another, be open and honest about your struggles and can ask each other the tough questions in an atmosphere of love, trust and non-judgement. Is this something you do? If not, could you consider doing?

Reaching out

Story

A young man was travelling through the countryside, hitching a ride when he could, but walking alone at other times. As dusk started to approach, he picked up his pace, trying to reach the next village in order to find a place to stay. Suddenly a group of thugs jumped him, punched him repeatedly until he was knocked to the ground, pulled a knife on him and demanded his iPhone and watch. Some of them kicked him while a couple of the others grabbed his rucksack and rummaged through it, grabbing anything they thought was worth taking. They then threw him into the ditch at the side of the road and ran off.

The poor man lay there, wincing in pain and unable to move. Every so often he was aware that others were passing by. A vicar cycled past, barely slowing down, intent on finishing his visits to his parishioners before night descended completely.

Next, a car travelled past, slowing down to look at what the strange object was by the side of the road. The woman, when she saw it was a beaten-up man, quickly sped up again, worried that her children might have seen him.

Finally, a man in a business suit spotted there was someone lying by the road, so stopped his car. He positioned his headlights so that he could see the person more clearly but wouldn't blind them with the light, and then gently called out. Discovering how badly the young man was hurt, he lifted him up, getting himself covered in blood, and laid him as gently as he could on to the back seat of his car. He used his own handkerchief and water bottle to wipe the young man's face clean, but realised he needed expert help.

The businessman drove carefully into the next village, stopped in the car park of the nicest looking pub and ran inside. He explained that he needed a room, asked the owner to call for a doctor and then went to fetch the young man. He asked the owner to help him carry the man to the room and then waited with him for the doctor. Once the doctor was finished, he explained to the young man that he would need to rest for a few days, and reassured him that he would be well looked after, and that he would be back to check up on him.

The businessman then gave his credit card details to the pub owner and asked him to look after the patient until he returned.

The above is my modern take on the story of the good Samaritan (Luke 10:25–37). I have chosen the characters that walked past on purpose, because they reflect how I can behave. With my children in my car I am much more protective and less likely to stop and help a stranger. And yet what am I teaching my kids through that, when I want them to be kind, merciful and loving to others? And what about the vicar? That reminds me that, even when I'm busy with what I feel called to be doing, I need to be open to those times God brings across my path people that need my care and attention immediately.

The biblical text has a Samaritan being the one who extended mercy to the injured man. To Jews, Samaritans were not pure because they were of mixed race; Jesus was turning their attention to how they could put piety over mercy. How well do you reach out to those that aren't within your own circle of friends? To those you find difficult? Could God be asking you to widen your definition of friendship and reach out to some different people?

Thanking God for your friends

Prayers

Use these prayers to focus on thanking God for your friends. The repeated line will help you with the reflective process. You may choose to read every line out, or read through them in your mind. Why not pen a few of your own lines too?

Friends
They stand by me through all circumstances of life.

Thank you, God, for friends.

They help me to see things from a wider perspective than my own.

Thank you, God, for friends.

They share their wisdom with me—and allow me to do the same for them.

Thank you, God, for friends.

They encourage me greatly.

Thank you, God, for friends.

They make me laugh and help me unwind.

Thank you, God, for friends.

They pray with me and for me.

Thank you, God, for friends.

They ask me the difficult questions.

Thank you, God, for friends.

They reveal a little more of your love for me.

Thank you, God, for friends.

Show your appreciation

Creative

It is great once in a while to show our friends practically how much we appreciate them. Pick one of your friends and spend some thinking about what would really help them; maybe choose a gift you know they would love receiving. I've put some suggestions below to help kick-start the process but feel free to use your own ideas. Start work on any of the handmade options you want to utilise today.

- Send a thank-you card through the post.
- Arrange for flowers to be sent to them.
- Buy them a special treat such as chocolates or a book.
- Invite them for a meal and then really pay attention to

cooking (or buying) one of their favourite meals, and creating a lovely atmosphere.

- Start a 'box of friendship' and, over the next week or so, collect things in it that you can then give as a present. You could also spend time decorating the box. The following are some ideas that you could either put in the box or use as stand-alone gestures of appreciation:

  * Little notes that explain why their friendship means so much to you.

  * Gifts (handmade or bought) that you know they will appreciate.

  * Bible verses that you feel God has led you to when you've been praying for them.

  * Handmade vouchers, such as 'this voucher entitles you to one free evening of babysitting', 'voucher for you and me to go to the cinema together this month', 'voucher for afternoon tea together'.

If at this stage of your life you feel lonely, ask God to bring people into your life who will be friends to you. Don't be passive: actively seek out how you can make friends with new people. Is there a hobby you used to enjoy that you haven't done for a while? Why not join a group in your community? Is there an area in your church you could serve in that you don't currently? Once you connect with people, reach out to them yourself in different ways—invite them for a coffee, have them over for a meal or take them to a restaurant. Above all, when they talk to you, really listen to them so that they feel valued and appreciated.

Abraham: hero of the faith

Amy Boucher Pye

The call

Introduction

God's promise to make Abram the father of descendants numbering as many as the grains of sand involves a great sacrifice on Abram's part—leaving his inheritance, his people, and all that was familiar to him as he became a stranger in a foreign land. He follows and obeys God, and later is cited in Hebrews as one of the heroes of our faith. As we delve into his story, you may wish to start by reading the parts we'll be looking at, which are in Genesis 12—13, 15, 16—18, 21—22 and 24, and Hebrews 11.

Today, as you consider God's call on Abram in Genesis 12:1–9, think about a time when you set off on a journey. One year, our family spent over a month in America, including a road trip of 2500 miles through which I introduced my British husband and children to the land of my birth—the rolling hills, friendly faces and small-town diners. Many memories stand out in my mind, such as joyous reunions, interesting museums and beautiful scenery. But I remember, too, the months of preparation for the trip, the weariness of sleeping in so many beds, the hours spent in the car watching the landscape pass by and the times of hunger and irritability. Our human frailties can play a greater part in how we travel than we might anticipate.

Abram and Sarai, at 75 and 65, leave their home to follow God's purposes and plans. Think back to a trip you took or a move you made, whether far from home or over to the next village. Prayerfully consider some of the lessons you learned and what you found out about yourself. Are you an adventurer or a homebody or somewhere in between? What new things about 'home' did you understand in the light of your travels? If you travelled with others, what did you learn about them? What struck you about the people you met?

God's call on our lives might prove costly. May we have pliable hearts and the faith to follow the Lord's leading.

Fear factor

Creative

I find the story of Abram in Egypt, when he passes off his wife as his sister, a tough one to read (Genesis 12:10–20). Abram lets his fears override his wisdom as in his mind he skips forward in time, believing that her beauty will lead to his death. In effect he gives her as a wife to Pharaoh, and thereby allows their marriage to be defiled. The Lord intervenes, sending diseases on Pharaoh and his house, and soon Sarai returns to Abram. I wonder how Sarai felt about the string of events.

As we reflect on this story, think about how fear can lead to lies and the consequences of being found out. We may think we can hide behind untruths, but of course God always knows—and often others find out too. Even lies told for the protection of others, or because we've promised secrecy, can wreak havoc in relationships.

Quiet yourself before the Lord, asking him to bring to mind any fears that might be lurking in your heart or sitting heavily in your gut. Write these out specifically on pieces of paper, naming them one by one. Offer your fears and papers to God, allowing him to be in them or to take them from you. Are you willing to let go? You may want to burn the papers (safely), to put them in the compost for the worms to consume or if you have a cross in your prayer space you may prefer to place the papers at the foot of the cross. Stay with God, receiving calm for these fears or the gifts he has for you to replace them.

A way through discord

Imaginative/intercession

Stuff can cause strife. As you read through Genesis 13, think about how the possessions of Abram and Lot got in the way of them living together in peace. Although the uncle and nephew may not feel a sense of discord in their relationship, their herders start to disagree about how things are done, and 'the land could not support them while they stayed together, for their possessions were so great' (Genesis 13:6, NIV). They need to find a solution. They agree to part, and afterward, Abram receives another promise from the Lord—a gift of land and offspring numbering like the dust of the earth. Out of heartbreak comes redemption.

Read through the story again, this time asking God to use your imagination to place you into the action. It could be as one of the major characters, or as one of those affected by the disagreement, such as a herder or a child, or as a bystander. Imagine what your character hears about the conflict and notice what you feel. Where do you end up? Who do you go with? How do those around you respond to the strife and to the solution? What's your new setting like? Where is God in all of this?

Take an area of conflict—it may be a situation you are involved with personally, or it may be a national or international item you have seen on the news. Ask God to show you how he could work and where he's already involved. Where do you see God's grace revealed?

Binding covenant

Creative

Genesis 15 is one of the standout passages of the Bible for me, in which the true and living Lord makes the promise to Abram that he will be the father of descendants numbering as many as the stars in the sky. As you read the narrative, notice just how much convincing Abram needs at times, such as when he says, 'What can you give me? … You've not given me children!' (vv. 2–3). The Lord seems to ignore his air of petulance, instead imparting Abram with the faith to believe.

This encounter marks a key point in Abram's journey to becoming the father of God's people. Step by step he moves forward in faith, growing stronger in the Lord and in the path of obedience. He is not perfect, and faces setbacks, but, as we will see, he is eventually credited as a hero of the faith, one who trusts and believes that God will follow through on his promises.

God put Abraham into the place where he could grow and become this hero of faith. So, too, seeds placed in the right place grow and become the flower, herb or plant they are intended to be. Find a pot or place outside to plant some seeds. As you prepare the soil, feel the earth and reflect on the places where you are planted. What does it feel like to be in them? As you bury the seeds in the soil, notice how you are immersed in various places. Allow God to be with you, and ask if there are things hidden in the earth waiting to grow. As you water your seeds, allow God to pour his living water over you.

As you tend your seeds and young plants over the coming weeks, notice the parallel work God does in your life.

Alternative plans

Bible study

We might find Sarai's suggestion (in Genesis 16) to Abram that her servant girl bear him a child strange, but in ancient times this practice was not only accepted but sometimes demanded by a marriage contract. The family line had to continue, and this was an acceptable practice to enable it to happen. But we're not surprised by the resulting breakdown in the relationship between Sarai and Hagar—Hagar turns on Sarai and lauds her blessing from the Lord, that is her pregnancy, over her mistress.

As you read Genesis 16, consider some questions. You might want to approach this exercise as a Bible study, writing down your answers and asking God to shed his light and wisdom, bringing you insight and understanding.

- What significance, if any, do you ascribe to Hagar's coming from Egypt, the land where the Israelites were enslaved?
- Hagar despises her mistress, and Sarai turns to Abram, blaming him. How does this negative spiral of relationships mirror what happened in the Garden of Eden between Adam and Eve after they ate the forbidden fruit?
- Hagar flees, but the angel of the Lord tracks her down. Why do you think the messenger of the Lord starts a conversation with her?
- How do you think Hagar felt when she received the word from the Lord about her son—that he would be a 'wild donkey of a man' and that he would 'live in hostility' (v. 12)?
- Read verse 13, and reflect on the power of seeing, and being

51

seen. Why do you think Hagar responded in this manner? When do you feel the Lord sees you?
- Does this passage inform your view of those outcast from society? If yes, how?

A new name

Reflective

In Genesis 17, the Lord reiterates to Abram his promise to make him the father of many nations, and also changes his and Sarai's names. No longer will he be Abram, which means exalted father, but Abraham, which means father of many. No longer will she be Sarai, meaning princess, but Sarah, meaning princess of many.

Read through Genesis 17, thinking about the change in names and the requirements God places on Abraham and Sarah as well as the promises he makes to them. You may like to spend time in prayer, asking God through his Holy Spirit to reveal if he has a new name to bestow on you. You could read Isaiah 62:2–5 in which the Lord promises to change the name of Israel from Deserted to Delighted In, and from Desolate to Married. Are there areas of your life in which a new name would help? Ask the Lord to bring his peace and love to you, that his everlasting arms may support you as you receive his affirming words.

Three visitors

Visual

Many Christians use icons to aid their prayers, seeing these unsigned paintings as windows to the divine; a gate from the visible to the invisible. Around 1410, St Andrei Rublev painted an icon commonly known as *The Holy Trinity* icon, depicting the story of Genesis 18:1–10a, when the three visitors—generally thought to represent the Trinity of God the Father, God the Son and God the Holy Spirit—came to visit Abraham and Sarah. You can easily find photographs of this icon online.

Read Genesis 18:1–16 with a copy of this icon before you. As you read, look at the icon and the characters depicted there.

The icon contains many symbols that are explained in various resources including Ann Persson's gentle exploration of this icon in *The Circle of Love* (BRF, 2010). Note how the three figures represent an invisible circle, a shape seen as a symbol of perfection, with no beginning or end; a circle which is open to the viewer. Note also that within the circle, the three heads of the figures form a triangle, which is a shape often used to depict the Trinity, and yet the three figures all have the same face, for as Jesus said, 'Anyone who has seen me has seen the Father' (John 14:9, NIV).

Continue to gaze on the icon as you ask God to reveal the word he has for you today.

The gift of laughter

Reflective

God follows through on his promises and, as we see in Genesis 21:1–7, he gives Sarah and Abraham a son, whom they name Isaac, which means he laughs. As Sarah says, 'God has brought me laughter, and everyone who hears about this will laugh with me' (v. 6).

We might think it far-fetched, but some people claim that laughter promotes healing. Around the world there exist laughter groups—those who come together for the sole purpose of laughing together. For laughter is an aerobic activity, strengthening the diaphragm and releasing endorphins, the feel-good hormone, into the body.

Whatever you think about laughter and healing, push yourself today to laugh more than usual, asking God to help release you from your inhibitions and embrace the joyful side of life.

Exclusion and embrace

Prayer/intercession

As we see in Genesis 21:8–21, there is more trouble in Abraham's household, as on the day when Abraham holds a feast to celebrate that Isaac was weaned, Hagar and Ishmael are expelled. Their taunts are too much for Sarah so she forces them out. Of course Abraham is upset, as Ishmael was his son. But the Lord reassures Abraham that he will care for his servant and son, even making Ishmael into a nation because he is Abram's offspring.

And so off to the desert again go Hagar and Ishmael. She must feel despair, for, fearing he will die, she moves away from her son, not able to watch. As you read the passage, reflect about the God of mercy who cares for the outcasts; who opens our eyes to the provision of water in the desert.

When thinking about this theme of exclusion and embrace (the name of a fine book by Miroslav Volf [Abingdon Press, 1994]), you may want to engage in a prayer exercise to name and release any places of desperation in your life. Are there times when you have felt like a foreigner or stranger, when you have felt like one who is removed from society and who doesn't belong?

Ask God through his Holy Spirit to show you any locations that hold particularly painful or awkward memories for you. If nothing comes to mind, that's fine—don't go digging. If something appears, ask the Lord to help you understand how to pray about it, such as showing you if you need to repent in any way, or if any sins were committed against you from which you'd like release. As you wait for God's word of peace and love, open your hands as a gesture to let go and to receive. Write down any images or words that come to you in the silence.

Alternatively, you could find a collection of small stones or pebbles. As you pray, arrange the stones into small groups. Then take one stone away, excluding it from the rest of its group. How does it feel to remove a stone, or for it to be removed? Where is God in this? Pray for those who are excluded and for those who do the excluding.

Laying Isaac down

Reflective

Read the famous story of God's testing of Abraham in Genesis 22:1–18, where God asks him to sacrifice his son, the gift and answer of many years of pleading and prayer. What do you think Abraham thinks and feels as he obeys the Lord's command? No longer does he take matters into his own hands, as he did when passing off his wife as his sister or fathering a child through his servant. Rather, at this point, his relationship with God has developed so that he heeds the Lord's instructions and sets off for the region of Moriah. Note also the conversation between Isaac and Abraham, for it mirrors the loving relationship between Abraham and the Lord. Just as Abraham trusts his heavenly Father, so too does Isaac trust that all will be well on this journey with his father. Similarly, as Isaac carries the wood on which he'll be offered as a sacrifice, so too does Jesus carry the cross on which he dies.

As you reflect on the passage, consider a few questions in the light of the story: What might be an 'Isaac' you need to lay down at the altar of the Lord? Is there anything in your life that could threaten to overtake your relationship with God as your primary source of love, affirmation and belonging? You could write down whatever comes to mind, setting it at the foot of the cross while you ask God to take his rightful place in your heart.

As you mull over the story, think also about how it reflects on God the Father as he sent his only Son to die in our place. How does this Old Testament story enrich your understanding of Jesus' passion story? Stay in that place between the Old Testament altar and the New Testament cross. What is God saying to you here?

Abraham gathered to his people

Reflective

Abraham has a good death, as we see in Genesis 25:1–11. As it says in verse 8, 'Then Abraham breathed his last and died at a good old age, an old man and full of years; and he was gathered to his people.' He bequeaths gifts to his sons before he dies, but leaves the full inheritance to Isaac, the son of the promise.

What gifts will you leave when you die? I'm not thinking of the money and goods you may have listed in your will, but rather that which will live on in others after you die. Spend some time thinking about what this might be. Offer it to God, asking how he wants you to use it while it is still yours. How can you serve God with it now? Thank God for the gifts he has given you and that you can pass these on to others.

May we, like Abraham, join the company of saints when we are promoted to glory.

Heroes of the faith

Prayer

I love Hebrews 11 and its list of women and men who believed what the Lord said would come true. By faith they lived and moved and had their being. By faith they welcomed the promises of God. By faith they were sure of what they hoped for and certain of what they could not see.

As we come to the end of our engagement with Abraham and Sarah, why not engage in a practice of *lectio divina*—sacred reading—with the parts of Hebrews 11 as related to Abraham. As we follow this ancient spiritual discipline of contemplative reading, we'll chew over the words and allow them to permeate to our inner being.

Read through Hebrews 11:1–3, 8–19. Read it slowly, allowing each word to have its time and space. Ask God to tune your heart to him, reading until a word or phrase strikes you. When that happens, stop with that word or phrase. Turn the words over and over in your mind and perhaps your mouth—the image used in ancient times for this was of a cow chewing its cud. As you repeat the words, let them interact with your thoughts, hopes, dreams and memories. Allow God's word to become his word to you, to become so much part of you that you can repeat it without hearing the words. As we ask God to change us, we allow his word to touch the deep places in our souls.

When you are ready, keeping in mind the word or phrase that struck you, respond to God. This may be thanksgiving, praise, petition, repentance or adoration as the prayer becomes a loving conversation with the Lord.

You may want to finish with a period of silence, turning off distractions and the inner voice that would have us rush off. It is enough to be and to enjoy. You can then return to the passage and read slowly until another word or phrase strikes you, depending on the time you have available.

After completing this exercise of sacred reading, you may want to reflect on this section and the lessons you've learned and insights you've gained from engaging with the lives of Sarah and Abraham.

May the Lord bless you in your journey to the heavenly country, whose architect and builder is God.

Music and prayer

John Fitzmaurice

Giving voice to prayer

Introduction

St Augustine famously said that when we sing we pray twice. This series of reflections will seek to explore the devotional and spiritual power of music and offer some ideas as to how you might harness it in your devotional life. There are two points worth making before we set out on this exploration. Firstly, I have tried to be as generic as possible in the suggestions of music you use. Sometimes it is necessary to be a bit more specific, but you can only make the best use of the music you have access to! The radio is a great source of music—Classic FM, BBC Radios 2, 3 and 6, and many other independent stations. Try listening to a station that you wouldn't normally hear. There is also a wealth of music on the internet via websites like Spotify. Have a look around and explore. You don't have to spend lots of money! Secondly, be brave with the exercises. You may not feel very confident musically, but this isn't your Grade 8 exam! God will honour your offering in prayer.

So, back to Augustine. Why did he say that to sing was to pray twice? If we are not careful, prayer can become a very cerebral activity. We can get caught up in our thoughts and our minds, even if it is only in trying to quieten them. What music does is to turn prayer into a physical activity, often just by listening. Music works kinaesthetically—we dance to it even if we are sitting still. Music speaks to our muscle memory, its tensions and releases. When we listen to or play music, our bodies, our muscles react unconsciously. This has a very profound effect and adds depth to our experience of prayer and the redemption of our whole selves, not just our intellect.

Sing a favourite song or hymn out loud. Try and hear how the shape of the music accentuates the meaning of the words. Really emphasise this, or even exaggerate it to make the point. Feel the unity of the words and music, the unity of your body and soul as you sing.

Lamenting

Listening

Since biblical times music has been an integral part of lamenting. A whole group of the psalms are known as Psalms of Lament. This tradition continues through the spirituals sung by slaves in American plantations, some of the protest music of the 1960s, and not forgetting Boney M's chart topping performance of the Psalm 137 'By the river of Babylon' in 1978. Popular songs are now routinely used at funerals both in crematoria and in churches, and serve as vehicles through which those who are grieving express their pain. 'Time to Say Goodbye' as sung by Andrea Bocelli and Sarah Brightman is a good example of this. There is something about grief that needs to be expressed more than simply in words. Our experience of loss and separation is often so visceral that it requires our expression of it to be visceral as well. The fact that music gets into the very fibre of our muscles means that we can express some very deep-seated emotions through it—emotions that our limited verbal vocabulary is unable to express.

Listen to a song of lament that is meaningful to you. It might be a song or piece of music that is attached to a particular individual in your life; it might be a piece that you would like played at your funeral or at the funeral of a loved one; it might be a piece that simply expresses some of the pain of the human condition, or a song about injustice. Enter into the physicality of the experience. You might want to stand up and see how your body responds when it has the freedom. How does your imagination respond? As well as impacting us kinaesthetically through our physicality, music also shortcuts our rationality— it allows our imagination to escape the censure of our egos and can help access deep truths tucked away in our mental imagination. Allow the music to draw you into a prayer of lament both physically and through your imagination.

Soothing

Listen/move

David played the harp to soothe King Saul (1 Samuel 16:23). The power of music to relax us is well known; a number of national radio stations are based on the relaxing power of music. This is a physiological response to what we hear. Our bodies have various natural rhythms; walking, breathing, our heart's beating. The more stressed we become, the faster most of those rhythms become. However, our bodies have an uncanny ability to connect to external rhythms, so in a large dance venue we feel exhilarated by the fast and insistent pounding of the music, and when we follow a marching band, it doesn't take long for our own walking pace to match that of the music. Slow music then can draw us back from a place of heightened emotion and into a place of calm and focus. For people of faith, if that slow music is combined with some words or at least music that resonates with our faith, then not only are we restored physically and emotionally, but also spiritually.

So select a piece of music that is slow and soothing. It's helpful if it is quite a long piece, as it can take a while really to settle into this process. If you are choosing music with words, choose something with a text that inspires or reassures. You might find that a chant from the Taizé Community or one by Margaret Rizza or some monastic plainsong is helpful. Sit or lie down in a position in which you can properly relax and, as you listen to the music, let your body rhythms join with the rhythm of the music. Don't force anything as that will only set up more tension—just let your body respond. You might prefer to walk slowly and meditatively to the pace of the music. To do this you might, if the surface allows, want to remove your shoes so you can feel the ground on which you are walking. Let the calmness of the music enter every fibre of your body, and soothe you.

Praising

Listen

Just as music can both soothe and enable us to lament at a deep level, so it can also empower us to praise in ways that go beyond words. Psalm 150 encapsulates this:

Praise him with trumpet sound;
praise him with lute and harp!
Praise him with tambourine and dance;
praise him with strings and pipe!
Praise him with clanging cymbals;
praise him with loud clashing cymbals!
Let everything that breathes praise the Lord!
Praise the Lord!

PSALM 150:3–6, NRSV

Music's ability to lift us beyond the mere verbal not only applies to situations of sorrow and lament, but also to those of great joy. There's always music at great celebratory events and when Christians want to celebrate and praise God, then music helps them in that endeavour. It's the other side of the soothing and lamenting coin. Fast, energising music can free us to express our excitement and enthusiasm for all that we have received, and yet there is also a form of praise bordering adoration that has a quiet, almost silent, intimacy.

How do you want to praise God? Do you want to praise loudly and vibrantly, or quietly and intimately? Both are fine. Different people do it in different ways at different times. Choose a piece of music that matches what you want to express. What physical posture might you adopt as you praise? Let the music help you express all the glory you want to reflect back to God and allow yourself to be carried away by it. When the music is over, just wait for a moment; don't just rush on to the next thing. Listen to the quality of stillness and silence that God has blessed your praise with. Wait in that silence and stillness and offer him all that you are and have.

Bringing down the defences

Reflective

A number of years ago there was an advertising campaign for a particular brand of lager that claimed it reached the parts that other lagers didn't. There's something in our experience of music that is not dissimilar. Music can penetrate the depths of our souls and psyches in a way that few other experiences can. The barriers that we consciously or unconsciously create within our memories, and behind which we hide difficult or painful experiences, can often be penetrated by music. Sometimes we can listen to music that feels like it cuts right into us and lays us bare. Frequently this experience involves tears, the tears of knowing ourselves known in a deep way—the knowledge that whoever created or composed this music, and whoever performed it, must have some inkling of the depth of experience that we too experience. This relieves us from our isolation and enables us to look behind the wall, behind the barriers.

In the Bible, Joshua used music to break down the walls of Jericho using trumpets, rams' horns and the shouts of the people (see Joshua 6). I wonder if there are areas of your life that you have barricaded off. What lies behind these barricades and why is it there? Does it need bringing to light for healing, for forgiving? Pray that God will reveal to you what is hidden in your life that he wants to heal at this time, and pray that he might reveal the right choice of music to assist you in this act. This is a difficult exercise because such acts of catharsis only happen by God's grace. We can't force them to happen, even by the choice of wonderful music! It might be that you need to do this a number of times, or it might be that such an experience will suddenly take you completely by surprise when you are least expecting it—God will use music to bring down your internal barriers and enable you to receive healing and forgiveness. If now is not the right time for you, be open to the possibility that God might use music in this way for you in the future.

Solo

Listen

We live in a world and indeed in a church where relationship is considered everything. We are expected to have lots of friends, if not real ones then virtual ones. Television advertising beams images of lots of happy, well-connected people into our living rooms on a daily basis. Relationship is important—the poet John Donne was correct when he said that no one is an island, and God calls us individually into a community of faith, where we journey together as a people. However, there is a danger in all of this if we begin to undervalue the worth of individuals and time spent on our own. An unbalanced and undiscerning focus on the collective can swamp the beauty and importance of the individual. Music has something of importance to offer us here. While much music making is of a collective nature, some of the most beautiful music is that of a single instrument or voice, or at least the interplay between an individual instrument or voice and a collection of other instruments and voices.

How can you make your life sing with the beauty of a soloist? A great instrumentalist puts hours and hours of practice into perfecting their art. Can you create a personal discipline in your life that develops and hones the particular skills and gifts that God has given you, and can you perform them in a way that gives glory to their creator? While it may not be everyone's cup of tea, the solo violin and cello music of J.S. Bach offers music of breathtaking complexity and beauty and shows what one instrument, what one individual, can achieve.

So find a piece of solo music to listen to, or even play, and just rejoice in the fact that you are who you are. Rejoice in your individuality; rejoice that God has made you unique; rejoice in the particular gifts and skills that he has given you for his service in the world.

Community

Reflective/creative

One of the ways we learn to play or sing is to do so with someone more experienced than we are, who can show us how it is done. This is what happens when we have music lessons: a more experienced teacher shows us how to do it, how to perform, and as we learn from them, we grow in confidence. We discover our individual voice through working alongside someone else and if they are a wise guide, they will encourage us to develop our individual sound and style, but to do so in a way that is compatible with the wider performance tradition.

This, of course, is how we learn and grow in faith. We need to come alongside others, to watch them, to imitate them, to listen to them, until we can find our own mode of practice and expression. This is why God calls us into community to a people of faith and not just a random collection of people with vaguely similar beliefs. We need each other because we learn from each other. Curiously, we discover our own individual voice by listening to the voices of others and selecting from what we hear that which resonates with our experience and from that selection we weave a distinctive sound.

So much music making is done in community. In many cultures, one of the primary expressions of community is communal music making. Think back on your life and recall those who have been instrumental in shaping you as the person you are today. From whom have you learnt your voice? To whose voice have you contributed? Listen to any music that involves more than one performer. Find a piece that really speaks to you and, as you listen to it, recall those different voices that have journeyed alongside you, taught you the faith, carried and supported you, those whom you have helped shape and support… and give thanks for them.

As you listen, draw a representation of those who have journeyed alongside you and how your paths have met and joined and separated. Let the music and drawing weave together.

Counterpoint (unity in diversity)

Reflective/creative

One of the truths of music making is that until we can hold a part on our own we are unable to perform with others. There is a paradox that means that in order to play or sing together, we must first be able to play or sing independently. This interplay between individuality and community is at the heart of musical activity; it is at the heart of our religious practice and indeed it is at the heart of what it means to be human. The musical device that best expresses this is called 'counterpoint' and refers to that form of music where different melodic elements interweave and blend with each other. Each line has a distinct melodic shape and is of equal value to the others. This is perhaps the ultimate expression of human community: a place where individuality is valued and encouraged, and yet is given context and shape by its engagement with all that is going on around it. Those performing counterpoint need to listen very carefully to those with whom they are performing to judge whether or not their melody is in the ascendant at any given time or whether they need to hold back and play a more supporting role for the time being and then move to the fore later.

How does your life interweave with the lives of others? How do you in your daily living craft and shape your God-given melody with those of others around you to create a beautiful whole? Listen, if you can, to some counterpoint, for example, the choral music of Byrd or Tallis or any of their contemporaries, or the fugues of Bach and his contemporaries. Reflect on the way your life is bound up with the lives of others and how you can yet retain your distinctive tune.

As you listen you might like to weave together some threads, wools and ribbons as you see your life and those of others interweaving.

Silence

Listen

I've often wondered what a visitor from outer space would make of our habit of clapping after a particularly wonderful musical performance. It seems to me that the performer spends a lot of time and effort creating a particular soundscape and just when they have completed it, we destroy it by banging our hands together. I think the reason we do this is because if we didn't, the subsequent silence would simply be too overwhelming—we wouldn't be able to cope with it.

It could be argued that all that music does is to shape the silence that follows it—sound emerges from silence and then returns to it. What would happen if, after a performance of Mozart's *Requiem*, we were to leave in silence and truly enter the ambivalence of the desolation of death and the hope of resurrection, or if we were simply to sit in silence for 20 minutes after hearing the profound simplicity of a work by Arvo Pärt? I would suggest that we are frequently scared of where music takes us and, rather than entering the depths of that place, we clap and quickly move on.

Today I want to encourage you to explore the silence that follows music. Choose a piece to listen to that you think has the potential to shape something profound. Make sure that nothing follows it. Sit quietly and listen to it and when it ends, simply carry on sitting. Enter deeply into the atmosphere, the silence, that the music has created and stay there fully absorbing its impact. What do you feel? How is this silence different from the one that might have preceded the music?

Creativity

Creative

Contemporary society is often characterised as a consumer society, in which everything is commodified and then sold. Music has not escaped this process. Gone are the days when music was primarily an activity done by everyone in the evenings at home or down the pub. Now we have highly paid experts (performers) who are the producers, and the rest of us are cast in the role of consumers. Some amateur music making survives in choirs, orchestras and bands of many kinds, but the performance of music by a wide variety of society has greatly reduced in recent years. For some societies such a situation would be unimaginable. In some ancient and indigenous cultures music exists only as it is performed—each performance is unique, and there is no divide between performer and listener. The notion of a recorded canon of music listened to outside the context of a community performance would simply make no sense.

If we believe ourselves to be made in the image of a creator God, then creativity will be a central characteristic of our humanity. Commoditisation risks destroying this aspect of our God-given humanity, but music is a means of retrieving it.

You might want to wait until everyone else is out before trying this activity or otherwise just let rip. Celebrate your God-given creativity by making a new piece of music. If you have access to an instrument, try using that, if not, just use your voice. Forget everything you think you know about what music should sound like, and just experiment! Try out a different range of sounds. Which ones do you like, which ones do you not like? Start to string them together. Do not judge your work—it's not a competition with Beethoven! Your piece will just exist for the moment in time that you play it and then it will cease to exist. Thank God for your ability to create even something very simple and give thanks that a little bit of your humanity is expressed through it.

As you perform for God, imagine his attention as he receives and rejoices in your humble offering.

Dance

Creative

Music has the potential to help us access the deepest levels of our humanity, to allow us to negotiate our personal individuality within the context of community and society, and through its kinaesthetic nature to unite our souls and bodies to allow a fuller expression of our experiences. Nowhere does this kinaesthetic experience manifest itself more than in dance. David controversially danced before the ark of the Lord (2 Samuel 6:14). It was controversial because it broke many of the conventions of his time, not least because it was the norm for women to do the dancing, and because he did so wearing only a linen ephod. Scripture makes clear that this was an act of thanksgiving and praise. This was no cerebral affirmation of propositional faith but an earthy, holistic offering of praise to a God in whom, David realised, the totality of his being was held.

As we dance, we conform our movements to the beat of the music, and as Christians, as we live, we seek to conform our lives to the heartbeat of God. Thus music and dance become the perfect analogy for our spiritual lives.

You might want to wait until everyone else is out… Choose some music that you find is really expressive. It may be fast and boisterous music (for example, Graham Kendrick's 'Teach me to Dance'), or it may be something slower and more reflective.

It can express whatever you want it to express—praise and thanksgiving, prayer, beseeching, contrition, and so on. Allow yourself to be taken up into the music and begin to respond to it by moving. Remember this is not an audition for *Strictly Come Dancing*—it is a way of trying to offer your whole self to God. Let go and let flow!

Celebrating

Listen

One of the temptations of sacramental faith is that things become a means to an end, they point to something beyond themselves, they become outward and visible symbols of inner and spiritual truths, and in a sense this is right and proper. We live in a sacramental world in which everything bears the imprint of and points us to our creator God.

This becomes problematic only when we can't look at a tree and see a tree, because we are immediately reminded of either Adam's sin in the Garden of Eden or Jesus' passion on the cross. I would suggest that sometimes God simply wants us to see and rejoice in the beauty of the tree!

Throughout these reflections we have been using music as a means of going deeper in prayer and into the reality of God, and the potential of music to enable us to do this is significant. However, I want to end by taking a less functionalist approach to music. God, of his bounty, gives a rich and abundant creation simply to enjoy—good food and wine, the smell of newly cut grass, the beauty of a sunset, human friendship and companionship... the list goes on. These things of course all point beyond themselves to the very nature of God, but that doesn't mean that they can't or shouldn't simply be enjoyed for themselves, just as they are—simple pleasures.

So, find some music that you love, play it loud, and thank God for the wonderful and extraordinary gift of music!

Treasure in jars of clay

Lisa Cherrett

Jars of clay

Introduction

'We have this treasure in jars of clay...' writes Paul in 2 Corinthians 4:7 (NIV). It's a passage in which he is urging the Corinthian Christians to persevere in their faith, trying to pass on his own joyful conviction that the light of the glory of the gospel of Christ overcomes the hardship of human life—even in a world that doesn't always recognise that glory or accept the gospel.

There are many avenues that we could explore when thinking about 'treasure' in the Bible, and many, equally, when thinking about 'clay'. The earthiness and fragility of humankind is pictured in various places in the Old Testament (such as Genesis 2, Jeremiah 18 and Psalm 103). Later, Jesus compared the kingdom of God with treasure—something worth searching out and selling everything for when it is found (see Matthew 13:44). Paul brings these ideas together in a stunning image of human life transformed by the power of God, and we shall be looking at several verses from chapters 2—4 of this passionate second letter to the Corinthians.

Before we launch off down some of those avenues, though, spend some time with the phrase 'treasure in jars of clay'. What do you imagine when you hear these words? What does the phrase mean to you? Paul means it to suggest a radical contrast. Treasure and clay jars are as unlike each other as they could be.

So why is it important to know that the glory of Jesus and the gospel is held in dull, ordinary, breakable vessels?

Walk around your house and garden and see if you can find some actual clay pots. What do they hold? Can you find any 'treasure'? Is it on display in your home, or is it hidden away somewhere? Why do you think this is?

Try to express in words or pictures—or other media, such as paint colours or fabric textures or music—the contrasts you see between 'treasure' and 'clay'. Ask God to reveal something new about 'treasure in jars of clay' as you explore the theme.

Made of dust

Reflection

What does Paul mean when he says we are like clay jars? First and foremost, clay jars in the ancient world were ordinary, everyday containers for all manner of contents—cooking ingredients such as oil and grain, as well as scrolls (the Dead Sea Scrolls were found stuffed into clay jars), wine and water (think of the enormous 100-litre jars in the story of the marriage at Cana in John 2:1–11). Clay would have been to biblical characters like plastic or cardboard is to us—cheap and plentiful, found in the homes of peasants as well as nobility, used in humble ordinary household tasks. Clay was, and is, an all-purpose material, made of common earth.

This should ring a biblical bell with us, echoing right back to Genesis 2:7, where God moulds the first human being (called Adam, or 'earth-creature') out of the dust of the earth. Perhaps that story was in Paul's mind as he wrote this letter to the Corinthians. In a sense, all human beings are made of clay, and we cannot escape its limitations ('dust you are and to dust you will return', says God in Genesis 3:19).

The story of our creation in Genesis 2 doesn't end there, of course. The earth-creature does not remain as earth alone. God 'breathed into his nostrils the breath of life [the spirit] and man became a living being' (v. 7). Therefore, every human being is a clay container filled with the treasure of the life breathed into us by God. Our physical bodies are not something shameful or embarrassing or second-rate (regardless of how we ourselves might feel about our outward appearance). They are, as Paul puts it in 1 Corinthians 6:19, 'temples of the Holy Spirit'.

Make a clay pot

Creative

Try making your own clay pot as an aid to your prayers over the next few days. You might use air-drying clay, Fimo® or Plasticine®. If none of these materials is available, you could make up some pastry dough to knead. Even a lump of Blu-Tack® or something similar would give you the feel of shaping clay. You could make a thumb pot by pushing your thumbs into the centre of a lump of clay and smoothing out the sides with your fingers, or a coil pot by rolling out long 'sausages' of clay and winding them round to make walls on top of a flattened base.

As you work, think of Jeremiah's visit to the potter (Jeremiah 18:1–4), where God spoke about the way he shapes and reshapes the lives of people and nations 'as seems best to him' (v. 4). You might think about what it means for the clay to be 'marred in [God's] hands' (v. 4): things go wrong for us; we are flawed in our own nature, and we are damaged by our life experiences and by other people's treatment of us. For some reason, God does not prevent this damage from occurring, but we can know that we never fall out of his potter's hands. He continues to shape us, calmly and purposefully.

When you're happy with the shape of your pot (or when you want to give up trying!), display it on a table or in some space that you could set aside as a prayer corner for the next few days. You may be adding objects to your display as you go on.

Grace in weakness

Meditation

Our physical bodies may not be shameful but they are fragile, and so is every aspect of our human life. We are like brittle clay in our minds and emotions, too. We are prone to all kinds of weakness, whether physical limitations or psychological difficulties such as anxiety, depression, addiction or other conditions that prevent us from living as full a life as we would like. The pressures of everyday life can wear us down, and not only as we reach more mature years. Isaiah 40:30 says, 'Even youths grow tired and weary, and young men stumble and fall.'

The messages we receive through the media tell us that we are of lesser value if we don't have a perfectly formed and functioning body and a strong, flawless mind. In the church, too, we can sometimes get the impression that the way we 'perform' is the most important thing about us. Do you look at the energetic worship leader on stage, the bestselling Christian author, the pastor of a thriving church or the national speaker with an amazing testimony, and imagine that they are the ones with all the treasure? If you are a tired parent, a 24-hour carer with restricted personal freedom, or someone with too much or too little work to do, perhaps you think of yourself as all clay.

Alternatively, perhaps you *are* an energetic worship leader, a bestselling Christian author, a pastor of a thriving church or a national speaker with an amazing testimony! If so, are you tempted to rely on your own strength, or do you sometimes feel hypocritical, afraid that your hidden weaknesses are about to be exposed?

From a Christian viewpoint, there is no shame in weakness. Even the apostle Paul had some kind of frailty that he was unable to overcome (his 'thorn in the flesh': see 2 Corinthians 12:7), which God refused to heal, so that Paul would rely on God's grace in his weakness. God 'knows how we are formed, he remembers that we are dust' (Psalm 103:14), and the treasure of the transforming Holy Spirit is available to all of us in equal quantity.

Cracked clay

Liturgy

Among the examples of clay pots that you found on your tour of house and garden earlier, did you find any that were chipped or cracked? Or perhaps you have a container that came as a 'second' from the factory? Place such an item in front of you. Touch and feel the imperfections. Hold the pot you made for yourself and feel how easily 'marred' it could be. Bring your physical, mental or emotional chips, cracks and breakages to God, using your own words or being guided by the prayer below.

Creator God, I bring to you the limitations of my body—
the bits that don't work perfectly, don't look great, don't stay strong for long enough.
You know how we are formed, you remember that we are dust.
Have compassion on me and give me your strength.

Father God, I bring to you the weakness of my mind—
the problems I can't solve and the anxious thoughts I can't settle.

You know how we are formed, you remember that we are dust.
Have compassion on me and give me your wisdom.

Redeemer God, I bring to you my fragile emotions—
the moods I can't control and the feelings that lead me into
deep trouble.
You know how we are formed, you remember that we are dust.
Have compassion on me and give me your peace.

What is 'treasure'?

Visual

What is the 'treasure' that Paul is talking about? He's writing
about spiritual qualities that are hard to describe in concrete
terms—'glory', 'power' and 'grace'. Indeed, he wants to stress
that in our life with Christ, 'we fix our eyes not on what is seen,
but on what is unseen' (2 Corinthians 4:18).

If I think of the 'treasures' I might find in my house, I think
immediately of certain pieces of jewellery, the old letters that
I keep in a box file, books that I've kept since my schooldays,
or photographs and journals. But Jesus said, 'Do not store up
for yourselves treasures on earth, where moths and vermin
destroy, and where thieves break in and steal' (Matthew 6:19).
All these 'treasures' of mine are prone to decay of some sort if
they are kept hidden away in boxes or are never moved from
their shelves: jewellery gets tarnished, and books and letters go
a bit yellow-edged and musty. Also, I realise that many of them
are reminders of the past—and the apostle Paul was supremely
uninterested in the past! His encouragements were always about
'pressing on towards the goal' (see Philippians 3:14).

Perhaps, to understand what Paul's idea of 'treasure' is, we
first have to consider and reject some of the things it is not. Do

we treasure some objects that are not really as valuable as we think they are? Many of our physical treasures are meaningful and beautiful in their own way and for their own time (see Ecclesiastes 3:11), but they are not the sorts of treasure that Paul is talking about here.

What are the treasures that you found around your house or garden? List them or place them physically in front of you. Speak to God about them, asking that they would find and keep their rightful place in your life, whatever that might be.

Treasure of endurance

Meditation

How, then, might we picture the treasure that Paul is writing about? There are several different ways, and we shall explore some of them over the next few days.

One clay jar that I found in my kitchen is a large one with the capacity to hold nearly two kilogrammes of rice. Rice is like bread or pasta or potatoes: it's a staple food, providing carbohydrates which are essential fuel for our bodies. They are converted into energy for life.

Paul talks about the 'treasure in clay jars' as something that gives us energy to endure, to fight through the hardships and obstacles that we encounter in our Christian lives: 'We are hard pressed on every side, but not crushed; perplexed, but not in despair; persecuted, but not abandoned; struck down, but not destroyed' (2 Corinthians 4:8–9). These verses remind me of Winston Churchill's famous 'Fight them on the beaches' speech, which comes to a climax with the words 'We will never surrender!' You can find a recording of the speech on YouTube if you want to remind yourself of it.

The Spirit of God in us sustains us and gives us strength and energy to endure the tough circumstances of life that threaten to overwhelm us. More than that, the Spirit enables us not just to endure but to overcome, getting up again every time we are knocked down.

In your prayer corner, place a heap of rice (or, if you prefer, some other starchy foodstuff such as bread, a handful of cereal or a potato). Thank God for the sustaining energy that is his spiritual treasure in the clay jar of your everyday human life.

Treasure of transformation

Visual

Another clay jar that I have at home is a plain, mass-produced terracotta plant pot of the type that you find piled high at the garden centre. I have only a small courtyard garden with two flowerbeds, so I make use of pots to increase my growing-space. The growth of a plant, from seed or bulb to green shoot, to bud and, eventually, to full flower (with new seeds then created from the flower), could be another picture of spiritual treasure—the slow but sure transformation that God causes to happen in us through our everyday lives.

Paul writes that we 'are being transformed into his image with ever-increasing glory' (2 Corinthians 3:18). The New Revised Standard Version of the Bible translates the latter phrase as 'from one degree of glory to another'. Each stage in the growth of a plant is glorious in its own way—it's certainly exciting to see the first tiny seedlings poking through the earth—but the colourful blossoms are the goal that the gardener is really hoping to achieve.

Could you find a small plant pot and a packet of seeds to place in your prayer corner? If you planted some seeds when looking at Abraham, go back to your seedlings. Enjoy them, noticing how they have grown, and what has changed over the weeks.

Meditate on the transformation that goes on in the shelter of the clay plant pot, and pray for a similar transformation from God in your own life. Are you at the stage of sowing seed for the future? Can you see new leaves or buds appearing in some kind of development of character or ministry? Is your life in full flower, or are you perhaps at the stage of harvest, producing innumerable new seed for future growth in yourself or in other people? What does God want to say to you or do in you, to move you to the next 'degree of glory'?

Treasure of fragrance

Visual

On the windowsill of my living room, possibly the warmest place in a relatively cool house, I keep three small rough clay jugs, unglazed and not decorated in any way. One quality of unglazed clay is that it's porous, so it absorbs oil and moisture. Into each of these jugs, I've poured a few drops of perfumed essential oils. The scents I've chosen are oils like amber, musk and sandalwood, which are used as base notes in perfumery. They are the scents that linger on, long after the flowery and fruity smells have faded away. My clay jugs remain scented for months or even years after being infused with these perfume oils.

In 2 Corinthians 2:14–15, Paul thanks God, who 'uses us to spread the aroma of the knowledge of him everywhere. For we are to God the pleasing aroma of Christ.' Then, in 3:11, comparing the new covenant in Jesus with the old covenant in Moses and the law, he says, 'If what was fading away came with glory, how much greater is the glory of that which lasts!' (NIV 1984).

The idea that we carry 'the aroma of Christ' in the clay jar of our ordinary lives in the world is an intriguing one, especially when you remember that our noses become insensitive to our own scent over time, even though other people will still be able to smell it. We may be unaware of the 'fragrance' that we bring into a room, but, if the transforming power of God is at work in us, that aroma—of the knowledge of Christ—can be spread wherever we go.

In your prayer corner you could include some kind of perfume. If you don't have any essential oils, some scented body lotion or shower gel would serve to remind you of this particular 'treasure'. In prayer, ask God to increase the attractiveness of his fragrance among the people you meet each day.

Glory

Creative

You might have noticed a word cropping up several times in the verses we've read from 2 Corinthians so far—the word 'glory'. When Paul writes of 'this treasure in jars of clay', he has just been explaining that God wants 'to give us the light of the knowledge of God's glory displayed in the face of Christ' (4:6, NIV).

What is this 'glory' exactly? In the Bible, the word often suggests a burning, dazzling light that accompanies the presence of God (for example, at the transfiguration of Jesus in Matthew 17:2, or on Mount Sinai, where Moses' face became radiant 'because he had spoken with the Lord': Exodus 34:29; 2 Corinthians 3:13). Few of us, I guess, will ever have seen such a phenomenon with our own eyes. Perhaps we have, ironically, only a very dim idea of what 'glory' would mean in our own experience.

Take a few minutes to meditate on the idea of 'glory'. Where do you think you've seen or heard something 'glorious'? There is a sense of excitement about the word. It suggests a vast expanse of brightness or a feeling of rising joy that overwhelms all other emotion. You might think of a burst of sunshine emerging from behind dark clouds, or the sight of an athlete suddenly putting on a spurt of speed to come from the back and pass competitor after competitor to win the race—in, as we might say, 'a blaze of glory'.

The piercing note of a brass instrument, such as a trumpet, might be described as a glorious, triumphant sound, but many other instruments and voices have also been used by composers to depict 'glory'. Try listening to the choral song 'O Radiant Dawn' by James Macmillan. (Possibly the best recording is available on YouTube: search for 'O Radiant Dawn #TheSixteen'.) Notice how the music seems to push outwards and upwards, as if it is swelling or pulsing with light.

If you wanted to describe 'glory' in such a way that another person might grasp its meaning better, how would you do it? Try to illustrate it using paints, collage materials or scraps of fabric, or design a flower arrangement. If you're brave enough, ask your church leaders if you could display your creation in church or at a housegroup meeting, with a short explanation of how it suggests 'glory' to you.

To show...

Meditation

What is the purpose of this treasure in clay jars? Is it for us to guard jealously, like the dragon Smaug with his horde of gold, or Gollum with his precious ring, in J.R.R. Tolkien's *The Hobbit* (HarperCollins, various editions)? If we know that God is full of generosity and self-giving love, then we will realise that his Spirit's power and glory are not for us to keep for our own benefit. The clue is in 2 Corinthians 4:7: 'We have this treasure in jars of clay to *show*...', and Paul goes on, '... so that his life may also be *revealed* in our mortal body' (v. 11, my emphasis).

The rice in my clay food jar provides energy for action; the flowers in my terracotta plant pot give a show of beauty to be enjoyed, nectar for bees to drink, and seed to guarantee future generations; the perfume oils in my porous jugs are meant to scent the room for all who come in. The glory of God is something that can't possibly be concealed. As Gerard Manley Hopkins puts it:

> *The world is charged with the grandeur of God.*
> *It will flame out, like shining from shook foil...*

Our instinct as human beings, when we know that we have 'treasure', something of enormous value, is to hide it away, perhaps even lock it away, to keep it safe. But, as I mentioned earlier, even with earthly treasures, this is often the wrong thing to do. Precious things that are not kept in use lose their beauty, their usefulness and their value. They fade, crumble, tarnish or rust. Most frustrating of all, we may even forget where we've put them for safe keeping.

With spiritual treasure, though, there need be no fear of loss or waste. We are free to be extravagant, like the unnamed woman who broke an alabaster jar of liquid nard and poured it over Jesus' head (Mark 14:3) or the widow whose jar of flour and jug of oil never ran empty as she continued to feed the prophet Elijah from them (1 Kings 17:15–16). How can you reveal the treasured life of God in you today?

Daily renewal

Liturgy

'Therefore we do not lose heart. Though outwardly we are wasting away, yet inwardly we are being renewed day by day' (2 Corinthians 4:16). Whatever condition we are in as 'clay', the 'treasure' of God's transforming grace and power is inexhaustible.

As you conclude your thoughts about treasure, thank God for the daily renewal of everything we need to reveal his life in the world.

Thank you, our Provider, for the unstoppable energy
you pour into us through your Holy Spirit.
When we feel weak, then we are strong:

therefore we do not lose heart.

Thank you, divine Gardener, for your transforming life
within us.
You watch over our growth from seed to flower:

therefore we do not lose heart.

Thank you, Creator of all things beautiful, that you help
us to spread the fragrance of Christ wherever we go.
You give us a peace that does not fade away:

therefore we do not lose heart.

Thank you, glorious Lord, for the dazzling light of
your presence.
Your radiance can break through the darkest of clouds:

therefore we do not lose heart.

Let your treasure be renewed in the clay of my life,
day by day. Amen

The Cloud of Unknowing—an introduction to contemplative prayer

Andrea Skevington

Going deeper with God

Introduction

The Cloud of Unknowing is a book written in the latter half of the 14th century—at a time of war and plague, when there was a great flourishing of spiritual works. Julian of Norwich, Eckhart, Catherine of Siena, Thomas à Kempis and Richard Rolle were all writing then.

Exploring this book has been such a rich experience for me. It has met my need for a different prayer approach—something quieter, and more transformative. I am only dipping my toe into these deep waters, but I hope we can learn something new, yet old, together.

It was probably written by a priest to a younger cleric, probably a monk. It assumes a grounding in Christian prayer and study, and a desire to know God who surpasses knowledge. It speaks to a need in our present age, a renewed interest in spirituality, in contemplation. Richard Rohr is one of the leaders of the new contemplative movement. Some of the material below is drawn from his talk at Norwich Cathedral (available on YouTube).

This book teaches its readers the principles of contemplative prayer, and we will go through some of these with exercises to lead us into the stillness of contemplative prayer.

Contemplative prayer

You may wish to establish a pattern for contemplative prayer, for example, turn off technology, find a place, light a candle, do some steadying breathing. Begin with this verse:

> *My soul thirsts for God, for the living God. When can I go and meet with God?*
> PSALM 42:2, NIV

Calm your mind. Let go of thoughts. Focus your loving attention on God, who is always present. Stay in the stillness, the silence, for as long as you can. When your mind wanders, try again.

Lift up your heart to God with humble love.
THE CLOUD OF UNKNOWING, CHAPTER 3

Love, not knowledge

Meditation

All rational beings, angels and men, possess two faculties, the power of knowing and the power of loving. To the first, to the intellect, God who made them is forever unknowable, but to the second, to love, he is completely knowable, and that by every separate individual... this is the everlasting miracle of love, for God always works in this fashion, and always will.

CHAPTER 4

In French, there is a distinction between *savoir* (to know a fact, a thing) and *connaitre* (to know a person). We are seeking something closer to the second, the love-knowing of relationship. Only when we lay aside our head-knowledge, and surrender to the mystery of eternal love, can we encounter God. Accepting this mystery is entering into the cloud.

> Reconcile yourself to wait in this darkness as long as is necessary, but still go on longing after him whom you love.
>
> CHAPTER 3

God's presence is represented as a cloud in the Bible. Exodus 13:21–22; 19:9; 40:34–38; 2 Chronicles 5:13–14; Matthew 17:5; Luke 9:28–36; Acts 1:4–9.

Take one of the passages listed above. Consider why cloud is used as a way of describing God's presence. Imagine yourself a witness to the event. What do you see? Do you wish to enter the cloud? What might that be like?

Contemplative prayer

> *We love because he first loved us.*
>
> 1 JOHN 4:19

Say this verse over several times, allowing your mind to quieten. Then, turn your attention to God.

> This is the marvellous unending miracle of love.
>
> CHAPTER 4

God alone

Creative

> Lift up your heart to God with humble love; and mean
> God himself, and not what you get out of him.
> CHAPTER 3

We are moving beyond gratitude, thanksgiving, praise, to loving
God, longing for God's own self. We are to 'mean God himself':
seek God with our whole being, moving from appreciating a
lover's attentiveness, gifts, kindness, and so on, to love for the
person themselves. We know we are often limited to thanking
God for..., but we seek to build a scaffold from those things to
the depth of God's own love.

> You must do likewise so far as grace enables you. Mean
> God wholly, and wholly mean God, so that nothing works
> in your mind or will but only God.
> CHAPTER 40

Read through the words of Psalm 131, slowly, and see how the
words resonate with *The Cloud*'s teaching. Let it still and quieten
your soul. Think what it means to be a weaned child. You could
write out the psalm and add your thoughts between the lines.

Contemplative prayer

Move on into the prayer of silent longing, seeking to know only
God for God's own sake. Notice what distracts you, and let it
fall away. Remember this is work, and takes effort.

So then love Jesus, and all that he has is yours. Knit yourself to him by love and faith.

CHAPTER 4

Be transformed by the renewing of your mind

Reflective

It can be hard to focus on an unseen God—our minds are so preoccupied. We can be afraid of letting go of thought, but we need to. For a while, we must learn to forget all but God, and to place a cloud of forgetting between us and all else, but God.

> Just as this cloud of unknowing is above you and between you and your God, so too you must put a cloud of forgetting beneath you and between you and all created things... In short, I tell you, everything is to be hidden under the cloud of forgetting.

CHAPTER 5

Our focus in prayer is often to bless, and lift people and situations to God in prayer. It can be hard to let go of that, and seek God alone. Try making space for intercession at other times, to free yourself to contemplate God and God alone.

Contemplative prayer

Read slowly several times:

> *Fear not, for I have redeemed you; I have summoned you by name; you are mine.*

ISAIAH 43:1

Become aware of the presence of God, who loves you. As intruding thoughts come, visualise them retreating into a fog, the cloud of forgetting. Focus your attention, as a 'dart of longing love' (Chapter 12), on God.

Time

Meditative/poetry

> God shows that time is precious, for he never gives two moments of time side by side, but always in succession... Love Jesus, and everything he has is yours. Because he is God, he is maker and giver of time. Because he is man, he has given true heed of time... unite yourself to him in love and trust.
>
> CHAPTER 4

The medieval mystics practised the discipline of dwelling in the now. We call it mindfulness, and think it is Eastern, but it existed in earlier forms of Christianity. We are to take our precious moments one by one, and remain in them, for it is in the moment that we encounter God, and grace. By spending time in the moment in contemplation, we can train ourselves to appreciate each moment, and to encounter God in these moments. You might find it helpful to look up 'The Bright Field' by R.S. Thomas.

Find a place—quiet or loud—and write down what you see, and hear, and feel, all around you. Notice details and how you respond. Record your thoughts and feelings. Aim to experience this moment as fully as possible. Let your writing flesh out this one rich instant. Give thanks for this moment now, now, now.

Set a reminder—hourly, or a few times a day—to notice God's grace and love in each moment.

Contemplative prayer

As you enter into the stillness, the cloud, set aside memory and anticipation, and share this moment with God. Stay for a few minutes.

The prayer of one word

Creative

> Why does it penetrate heaven, this short little prayer of one syllable? Surely because it is prayed with a full heart, in the height and depth and length and breadth of the spirit of him that prays it.
> CHAPTER 38

The Cloud assumes we pray with words, and takes us deeper, quieter, to prayers of near silence—simply the direction of our attention to God. A single word prayer, ideally a single syllable prayer, is seen as helpful, though, in our stillness. 'Short prayer penetrates heaven.'

We are perhaps used to thinking of a mantra as something from Eastern mysticism. Here we see our own contemplative tradition offering something similar—something that focuses our mind, and our heart, on God, and allows us to direct our attention on God while quieting our restless minds.

Its roots go back even further, to the Hebrew name for God Y-H-W-H. A word of two syllables, this is a word that can be breathed rather than said—'Yah' on the in-breath and 'Weh' on the out. The tongue and the lips do not close or block the breath when the word is breathed. Taking one word as a focus for meditation can be very helpful. You can use the list below, or any other words which speak to you.

You could write the word at the centre of a piece of plain paper, and then draw, colour and write around it in a kind of holy doodling. You could write or paint a word on a stone and hold it while you pray, or hold the word in your mind while you commute, walk, or do work with your hands. Some suggestions: anchor—growth—challenge—joy—edge—flourish—goodness—wild—other—yield—love—wind

Contemplative prayer

Seek stillness, reminding yourself that you are here to learn how to love—God and others. Turn your loving attention to God, who loves you. Use your word to help you. If this becomes a pattern for you, you may find that the saying of the word, under your breath or in your mind, helps bring you back to this place in times of difficulty.

Love and penitence

Imaginative

For our Lord said to Mary Magdalene, the typical representative of sinners called to the contemplative life, 'thy sins be forgiven thee'. Not for her great sorrow: not for her anxiety over her sins; not for her humility as she contemplated her wretchedness; but surely, because she loved much.

This is the point where we can see what secret and urgent love may obtain from our Lord; far beyond anything we could imagine.

CHAPTER 16

The Cloud considers Mary at some length, but it unites figures we might see as separate: the unnamed woman who anoints

Jesus, Mary Magdalene, and Mary sister of Martha. Perhaps we can identify a 'Mary spirit': a faithfulness, an extravagant love, a desire to be close to Jesus. May we develop such a spirit.

The Cloud warns of the dangers of dwelling on sin, rather than the love of God. We are encouraged to see our sin 'as a lump', rather than repeating our worst moments in our imagination. Here, we read, 'Did she descend from the heights of her longing to the deeps of her sinful life to search in the filth and sewage of her sins, fetching them up... brooding and sorrowing and weeping? Of course she didn't!' Such a course was seen as a dangerous, false piety. A focus on sin was seen as far more likely to lead to more sin and to despair.

So, she 'pinned her love and her longing desire to this cloud of unknowing', not understanding how Jesus could accept her, but longing that he would, both lost and found in this love for him.

Read Luke 7:36–50 through, imagining what it must have been like to be there. What can you see and smell and hear? Flickering lamplight? The spices? Who else is there? Read again, slowly, imagine you are hiding in the background, with a gift for Jesus. You are afraid of Simon the Pharisee, but your longing to kneel at Jesus' feet is greater. See this as the dart of longing love, which finds its mark. Kneel at the feet of Jesus, and pour out what you have to him.

Suggested music: 'Alabaster', Rend Collective
(www.youtube.com/watch?v=YILseGtYVVE)

Contemplative prayer

Stay at the feet of Jesus, wordlessly pouring out your love, and knowing that you are accepted.

Martha and Mary—action and contemplation

Creative

> But what she was looking at was the supreme wisdom of his Godhead shrouded by the words of his humanity. And on this she gazed with all the love of her heart. Nothing she saw or heard could budge her, but there she sat, completely still, with deep delight, and an urgent love eagerly reaching out...
>
> CHAPTER 17

Mary sits at Jesus' feet, among the disciples, and does not help Martha with the preparations. *The Cloud* explores the tensions that can arise between action and contemplation. When asked which was most important, Richard Rohr replied 'and'. We are not to judge those who choose either path. If we are called to contemplation, we are to pursue it. We will see that it teaches us to love, and so is the source of virtue and goodness. Without such love, good actions can flow out of anxiety, pride and self-righteousness, rather than compassion and humility.

Other spiritual writers, such as Brother Lawrence, write of maintaining the presence of God in the midst of activity: 'The time of business does not differ with me from the time of prayer; and in the noise and clatter of my kitchen, while several persons are at the same time calling for different things, I possess God in as great tranquillity as if I were on my knees' (Brother Lawrence, *The Practice of the Presence of God*, Merchant Press, 2009).

Read through Luke 10:38–42 slowly, imagining yourself present at the scene as richly as possible. Put yourself in the place of Mary, and then reread in the place of Martha—what are they feeling, and thinking? How are they both demonstrating love for Jesus? Can we re-imagine being Martha—a Martha who turns all things into prayer and contemplation?

Contemplative prayer

Come to a place of stillness, sitting at Jesus' feet, waiting for him to speak. Seek to let nothing budge you or distract you.

Temptation and its remedies

Reflective

> If memories of your past actions keep coming between you and God, or any new thought or sinful impulse, you are resolutely to step over them, because of your deep love for God; you must trample them down under foot. Try to cover them with the thick cloud of forgetting...
>
> CHAPTER 31

Remembering past wrongdoing, and being tempted to future wrongdoing, are treated the same in *The Cloud*—both come between us and God. The first remedy suggested is the cloud of forgetting—letting the thoughts retreat into the fog. We quickly move on to replacing those thoughts with something else: 'Try to look, as it were, over their shoulders, seeking something else, which is God' (Chapter 32). Remembering the profound love of God is the best remedy for temptation.

We seek to return to a pure hearted focus on God, and the contemplation of his love. We are to be people rooted and grounded in love.

Such people know that if they have God they have all good, and therefore they long for nothing in particular, but only good God.

CHAPTER 40

Bear with each other and forgive one another if any of you has a grievance against someone. Forgive as the Lord forgave you. And over all these virtues put on love, which binds them all together in perfect unity.

COLOSSIANS 3:13–14

Rather than focusing on the things we should avoid, we seek instead the way of love. So today, let us put on love. If critical, judgemental thoughts occur to you, let them fall away into the cloud of forgetting. We will seek to live this day in love and acceptance, keeping our eyes on God.

Contemplative prayer

We must therefore pray in the height, depth, length and breadth of our spirits.

CHAPTER 39

As you quiet, remember that the love of God is filling you. What a way to grow in our capacity to love! Focus your attention on God, knowing God loves you.

Let this thing deal with you

Going out

Let this thing deal with you, and lead you as it will. Let it be active, and you passive... Be the tree: let it be the

97

carpenter. Be the house, and let it be the householder who lives there... It is enough that you should feel moved lovingly by you know not what, and that in this inward urge you have no real thought for anything less than God...

CHAPTER 34

This process, of waiting on God, allows the Spirit to work deeply in our hearts. We submit to this loving work of God in our lives. It is hard, and humble, and transforming. 'All holy desires grow by delays' (St Gregory, quoted in Chapter 75), and so our uncertainty, our unknowing, can help us to grow our desire for God alone, and to be transformed by the work of the Spirit. This is the dart of longing love, that can pierce the cloud of unknowing, and bring us to a place of union with God.

> *I wait for the Lord, my whole being waits,*
> *and in his word I put my hope.*
> *I wait for the Lord*
> *more than watchmen wait for the morning,*
> *more than watchmen wait for the morning.*
>
> PSALM 130:5–6

Perhaps spend some time outside, or looking through the window, watching the sky. Notice patterns of cloud, and sunshine. Notice how light penetrates the clouds, riming them with silver. If you are awake early, wait for the morning and the first light of dawn. Notice how light changes everything.

Contemplative prayer

Use the words of the psalm above to draw you to longing for God, as we long for the light of dawn. Wait and long.

Virtues all flow from love

Meditation

> For virtue is nothing but an ordered, deliberate affection,
> plainly directed to God, for his own sake. How? God in
> himself is the pure cause of all virtues.
>
> CHAPTER 12

Goodness comes from God. 'However much you might weep in sorrow for yours sins', goodness cannot be obtained that way. If we fix our hearts on God, we will become soaked through with goodness. 'Negatively, it destroys the ground and root of sin, and positively, it acquires virtue. For if this love is there in truth, so too will all other virtues truly, perfectly, and knowingly, be included in it.' This wisdom has its roots in the words of Jesus:

> *'Love the Lord your God with all your heart and with*
> *all your soul and with all your mind.' This is the first*
> *and greatest commandment. And the second is like it:*
> *'Love your neighbour as yourself.' All the Law and the*
> *Prophets hang on these two commandments.*
>
> MATTHEW 22:37–40

'If you want to be holy, be kind,' said Frederick Buechner (American theologian and writer; quote from http://www.christianquotes.info/quotes-by-topic/quotes-about-kindness/#participants-list). Think how transforming this love would be in your community, your church, your workplace.

Read 1 Corinthians 13:1–12 slowly in the light of all you have learned and experienced of contemplative prayer. Notice that love is at the heart of all good. Noble and pious action without love springs from self. Love is the fundamental truth which endures. Notice the words which call our attention to the good. Linger over verses 11–12. Consider what they might mean for you. Remember the ancient mirrors are polished metal—they give a cloudy, diffuse reflection. As you read, how are you seeing God? The book tells us to 'beat away at this cloud of unknowing between you and God with that sharp dart of longing love' (Chapter 12). It can help to think of it as a loving gaze, seeing through all obstacles, forgetting all else but the beloved. We can pray that we may see God with the eyes of our hearts, truly.

Contemplative prayer

Then I shall know fully, even as I am fully known.
1 CORINTHIANS 13:12

Focus your attention on God, even through the cloudiness of an imperfect mirror. Remember you are fully known, and fully loved. Seek to know and to love in return. It is in the cloud that such an encounter takes place. Even though we cannot understand God with our minds, we can know him through the experience of love.

Loving action—practice the holiness of kindness today, being open-hearted to those you meet, and generous in your thinking and speaking of others.

If you are facing a difficult situation, let love be your guide.

Changed

Creative

Nevertheless, in this work of loving God, he has no time to consider who is friend or foe, brother or stranger.
CHAPTER 25

Although the practice of contemplation is often solitary, its impact is communal. An increase in love, and a decrease in judgement, ripples out to the benefit of all. *The Cloud* reminds us we are all one body and will seek to alleviate another's ache which pains us too. The one who is transformed by the love of God will show that love in their face and in their actions. They will be at home in any company, as Jesus was, and rather than be led astray, will lead others to goodness (Chapter 54). To be transformed is to show, by love and wisdom, how others too can be transformed. This love and goodness is attractive to our deepest and truest natures, and people are drawn to it.

> All who engage in this work of contemplation find that it has a good effect on the body as on the soul, for it makes them attractive in the eyes of all who see them.
>
> CHAPTER 54

Loveliness comes from love. God's love delights us. In seeking God alone, we are strengthened to love, even the unlovely. We remember the crowds who followed Jesus. We remember how Jesus spoke of drawing all to himself. This is the way of love.

> For charity is nothing else than loving God for himself, above all created things, and loving men in God just as we love ourselves.
>
> CHAPTER 24

Find something broken—either something of yours, or something belonging to someone else (with permission)—and mend it, or find something old and tatty and do it up. As you do so, think of being changed, made better, restored. Think of God doing this work in you.

Consider ways in which you could love and serve others, in

particular those whom you find hard to love, maybe people you disagree with or who are very different from you. Pray for them, and seek their good.

Contemplative prayer

> *Be still and know that I am God*
> *Be still and know that I am*
> *Be still and know*
> *Be still*
> *Be*
> (BASED ON PSALM 46:10)

Still yourself before God, who loves you. Turn all your heart to God, and be open to receiving this love.

He asks no help, but only you yourself.
CHAPTER 2

Sources: *The Cloud of Unknowing and other works*, Penguin Classics 1978
The Dart of Longing Love: daily reading from The Cloud of Unknowing, Darton, Longman and Todd 1983.

Some prayers in the Old Testament

Jean Sims

A promise from God

Introduction

As it was in Old Testament times, so it is today: God longs for us to join in the two-way communication between ourselves and God, expressed in prayer. Israel has a collection of written prayers in the Psalms, but we shall be exploring some prayers recorded in other books of the Old Testament. These prayers happen in the midst of narrative; in the midst of life, sometimes at a time of crisis and sometimes in everyday routine. They are prayers of individual people, with different ways of speaking and listening to God, and they can become our prayers. Through them we can understand more about God and how it is possible to encounter and grow into a deepening relationship with God.

So, begin by hearing God speaking to you in the promise given in Jeremiah 29:12–14. Repeat it several times, letting the words sink deeply into you, as you place your own name into it, making it your own.

'When you (*your name*) call upon me and come and pray to me, I will hear you. When you (*your name*) search for me, you will find me; if you (*your name*) seek me with all your heart, I will let you find me' (NRSV).

Prayer as a conversation with God

Imaginative

Moses was going about his everyday routine, tending the flock of his father-in-law. As he came to the far side of the desert, something caught his attention. There was a bush on fire, but it was not burning up. When he moved nearer to look more closely, he had an unexpected meeting with God. This experience and the conversation he had with God changed his life.

Imaginative contemplation is a way of entering into this story more deeply with the heart as well as the head, allowing the God, who is with you today, to speak to you in a fresh way.

Carefully read Exodus 3:1–15.

Then, putting your Bible aside, ask God to be with you as you begin to imagine the scene. Do not be too concerned about seeing the desert exactly as it was; it is being open to God at this moment that is important. You may find that you are watching the scene as yourself, or that you become Moses, or a companion, or you may shift from 'becoming' one person to another as the story unfolds. Maybe you will even see it from God's point of view. Just go with the flow. It is all in God's keeping.

These prompts might help: in your imagination, picture the scene, noticing what you can see, hear, touch and smell; the weather and the time of day. Moses is there looking after his flock, searching for places where the animals can find food and water. How is he feeling? What is he thinking? As he scans the horizon, he sees the strange sight of the bush, which is on fire but is not burning up.

As he goes to investigate, he hears God calling to him from within the bush. How is Moses feeling? How do you feel? Listen to the conversation, maybe joining in if you feel God speaking to you and, if you have a sense of awe, worshipping.

When the conversation is over, and when you are ready, thank God and return to the present.

Talk to God the Father or to Jesus or to the Holy Spirit about what has happened, responding through your feelings or in words.

Prayer as a reasoning with God

Reflective

Read Numbers 14:10–20.

Yet again, the people, whom Moses was leading towards the promised land, have rebelled. Moses goes into the tent of meeting and has an open and frank conversation with God.

God sounds exasperated with the people. 'How long will these people treat me with contempt? How long will they refuse to believe in me in spite of all the miraculous signs I have performed among them?' (v. 11, NIV). They deserve punishment. Moses then points out to God that the surrounding nations will not believe in God's power and intimacy with the people if he destroys them (vv. 13–16). He then quotes God's own words back to God (Exodus 34:6–7), reminding God of who God has said he will be. Moses pleads, 'In accordance with your great love, forgive the sin of your people, just as you have pardoned them from the time they left Egypt until now' (Numbers 10:19). God listens to Moses, 'I have forgiven them, as you asked' (v. 20). God and Moses are friends who can confide in each other.

Think about your own relationship with God. Are you confident enough to speak with God honestly, as a friend? Can you plead for forgiveness for others? Talk with God about it.

Praying while disobedient

Imaginative

Jonah was sent by God to 'preach against' the wicked city of Nineveh (Jonah 1:2). However, Jonah disobeyed and took a ship in the opposite direction. 'Then the Lord sent a great wind on the sea, and such a violent storm arose that the ship threatened to break up' (v. 4). As the sea was 'getting rougher and rougher' (v. 11) and 'wilder than before' (v. 13). Jonah told the sailors to throw him overboard. When at last they did so 'the raging sea grew calm' (v. 15). 'The Lord provided a huge fish to swallow Jonah' (v. 17), even though he had not prayed for help or repented of his disobedience. Being in the great fish did not guarantee Jonah's safety. It was not a pleasant place to be and he was still in a state of rebellion.

It was while he was inside the fish for three days and three nights that Jonah prayed his prayer of thanksgiving.

Read Jonah 2.

Jonah is thanking God in anticipation that his rescue will be completed. Despite being in a state of rebellion and disobedience, he can turn to God, because he knows who God is. He has come to his senses. Jonah can vividly recall his terrifying experience in the water and thank God that he is no longer there. He no longer clings to 'worthless idols' (v. 8) but thanks God for his rescue. For Jonah, the worthless idol may well be his own stubbornness and disobedience, putting himself above God.

Read this chapter again, imagining the storm as described by Jonah. Hear and see the wildness of the storm—the water heaving, the wind howling, the waves crashing. Feel the water and Jonah's panic. There are pictures and sounds of storms at sea on YouTube which could help with this, or you could play some music, like the fourth sea interlude from Benjamin Britten's opera *Peter Grimes*, or the overture to *The Tempest* by Sibelius.

Remember Jonah's conviction that God will rescue him and give thanks that the God who rescued Jonah, despite his disobedience, is the same God who hears us and acts in our lives in our times of disobedience, as well as in our times of obedience.

Prayer as being available for God

Contemplative/creative

Read 1 Samuel 3:1–10.

The boy Samuel heard someone calling him, and it was only when Eli told him that it was God calling, and how to respond, that Samuel was able to hear God clearly.

Allow a set time for this prayer; for however long you are comfortable with silence, or have time available, perhaps two minutes, five, ten or longer. So that you do not have to think about the time, set an alarm, gentle sounding if possible. Sit with your hands open on your lap, palms facing upwards. Use Samuel's words, 'Speak, Lord for your servant is listening' (v. 9).

Then continue to sit quietly with open hands, being available for God. If you find silence difficult, repeat Samuel's words, or something similar like, 'Here I am, ready for you.' When your time for this has finished, thank God. God has been with you in the time even if you have not been aware of the presence.

Another response could be to draw round your open hands on to some paper. Use different coloured pens or pencils slowly to write Samuel's words on the hands again and again, making them your prayer as you do so.

Samuel needed Eli's help to recognise that it was God calling him. If you feel that God is calling you to something, but it is not clear, talking in confidence with someone you can trust could help.

Prayer for wisdom

Intercession/going outside

Read the account of Solomon's prayer for wisdom in 1 Kings 3:5–15.

He came to his throne through violence and intrigue, but in his dream he saw himself differently, as someone who needed God's gift of a 'discerning heart' in order to 'carry out his duties' to govern well 'and to distinguish between right and wrong' (vv. 7 and 9). He does not ask for long life or for wealth, but for the wisdom necessary to govern fairly and do a good job of work. In his dream, God is pleased, gives him a wise and discerning heart and added to that, 'riches and honour' (vv. 12–13). Also, if he lives God's way, he is promised a long life (v. 14). When Solomon wakes, he realises that it is a dream, but within that dream is a profound reality of an encounter with God. Solomon has touched into the deep desires of his heart and has met God there.

Ask God to show you the deep desires of your heart, which come from God, and dare to dream that God will fulfil them.

As we all need wisdom each day, pray to God with short 'arrow prayers' for wisdom for each person who is part of your life today, especially those you pass or meet as you go outside. Remember too all those, such as refuse collectors, post people and road menders, who maybe are seen only by the jobs they have done. If you are housebound, travel round outside in your imagination. Ask God to help you notice those who need this silent, secret prayer.

Prayer as responding to the holiness of God

Meditative

Isaiah was in the temple 'in the year King Uzziah died' (Isaiah 6:1). For Isaiah and the country, this meant a time of change and uncertainty. Uzziah had reigned for 52 years and during that time had strengthened the kingdom, improved the defences of Jerusalem, had built up a well-trained and equipped army and provided shelter and water for his agricultural workers, 'for he loved the soil' (2 Chronicles 26:10). Above all he tried to follow God and was wise enough to accept guidance from another. 'He did what was right in the eyes of the Lord... He sought God during the days of Zechariah, who instructed him in the fear (vision) of the Lord' (vv. 4–5). It was only towards the end of his reign, when 'his pride led to his downfall' (v. 16) and he was seen as unfaithful to God and became a leper, that he was relieved of his responsibilities.

So Isaiah came into the temple probably full of memories of the old king, his faithfulness to God and then the character fault, which led to his tragic end. Although the new king Jotham had been regent at 25 years old, he must have appeared young in comparison to the experienced Uzziah, who was 68 when he died, so now there was the uncertainty of the new king's reign and the possibility of the political upheaval that often accompanies a change of ruler. As well as this we are told, 'The people continued their corrupt practices' (2 Chronicles 27:2). So, in the midst of this, Isaiah goes to the place where he knows God is to be found.

Now slowly and carefully read Isaiah 6:1–8.

With your body comfortable, and leaving aside any concerns you have, relax into prayer. Join the calling of the seraphs (v. 3) by repeating their words several times, slowly and reverently.

> *Holy, holy, holy is the Lord Almighty:*
> *The whole earth is full of his glory.*

As you worship God, you might find that 'Holy, holy, holy' is enough. When you are ready, let the words die down until you are with God in silence, savouring God's presence.

Stay in the silence.

Does God lead you into any other response? You might spend the time quietly enjoying being in God's presence in thankfulness or singing or shouting aloud in joy, moving as you do so. You might come to a deeper knowledge of your own humanity; or you might sense God calling you to something new or maybe to continue faithfully in the way you are living now. Be willing to let God lead and gift you.

Songs of praise (1)

Imaginative

There are two songs of praise as part of the prophecy in Isaiah 12, which speak of the joy that will be felt when the Hebrews return to their own land after a time of exile. They are also songs that we can pray for ourselves, in our own circumstances.

We start with the first song in verses 1–3. Read the first two, which are written in the first person. Notice that they praise the Lord for the way in which he has forgiven and comforted. Then the Lord is affirmed as the one who saves and therefore can be trusted without fear. He is 'my strength and my song' (v. 2).

Pause for a moment.

Say, 'I will praise you, O Lord.'

Now think of some characteristics of God, like his faithfulness, compassion, mercy… and say, 'I praise you, O Lord, for your faithfulness. I praise you, O Lord, for your compassion.'

Continue praising in this way.

Now, remember a time when the Lord has forgiven and comforted you and give thanks. Perhaps there is something for which you need to ask forgiveness now. God is looking on you with compassion as you do so.

Is there something for which you are fearful for yourself, or for others, and for which you need to trust God? After sharing it with God, in the belief that in love, God knows and understands you completely, you could pray part of verse 2, 'I will trust and not be afraid', or, if that is too difficult at the moment, change the words to 'Please help me to trust and not be afraid.'

Then comes the promise from God, 'With joy you will draw water from the wells of salvation' (v. 3).

Again pause for a moment.

Imagine that you are hot, tired, dry and thirsty. You find a deep well full of cool refreshing water. How do you feel? You lower a bucket on a rope and carefully fill it with water, pulling the now heavy bucket steadily to the surface. Now you have the water! You plunge your hands into it, filling them with thirst-quenching water to drink. Again and again, drink the water, tasting its freshness. There is an abundance of water, so now you can pour it over yourself, rejoicing as it cleanses and renews your tired body.

Remember the promise, 'You will draw water from the wells of salvation.'

Songs of praise (2)

Creative

The second song of praise in Isaiah 12, in verses 4–6, seems to be from the thankful hearts of all God's people. They thank God, call on his name and then share what glorious things God has done. They encourage each other to make known not only what

God has done, but also to tell all the nations of the world about the kind of God they are worshipping. God is great. God acts. It is as if they cannot help themselves. The knowledge of what God has done is so marvellous that they cannot keep it secret.

Pause again.

How might you make these verses your own? These suggestions might help.

How could you, and those with whom you worship, encourage each other?

One way would be to make a point of affirming fellow worshippers by what you say, text or write to them.

In the wider Church, get information from Christian mission organisations and aid agencies, who show the practical compassion of God. Respond to this information through prayer, practical giving or letters of encouragement.

How might you respond in praise?

Do you want to praise with others? Look for someone.

Even if you are on your own, your praise is part of that of the whole Church, the communion of saints.

If you are finding it difficult to praise, repeat verse 1, 'I *will* praise you, O Lord.' Use coloured pencils or pens to write the words out on paper or card and put this where you will see it for the rest of the day. You could ask, 'Please help me to praise you, O Lord,' and then start naming things for which you can give thanks and praise.

Praying in a political crisis

Intercession/creative

Read 2 Kings 19:15–19.

Hezekiah, the king of Judah, was in trouble. Sennacherib, the powerful king of Assyria, had captured the northern kingdom of

Samaria and was moving south through the country of Judea, taking all the fortified cities as he marched towards Jerusalem. Hezekiah had tried to persuade Sennacherib to withdraw by paying him a huge amount of silver and gold, as the Assyrian king had demanded. Despite this, Hezekiah eventually received a threatening message from him saying, 'Do not let the god you believe in deceive you, when he says, "Jerusalem will not be handed over to the king of Assyria." Surely you have heard what the kings of Assyria have done to all the countries, destroying them completely. And will you be delivered?' (vv. 10–11). Sennacherib seemed unstoppable.

When Hezekiah had read the letter, 'he went up to the temple of the Lord, and spread it out before the Lord' (v. 14). Now read Hezekiah's spoken prayer in verses 15–19. His action in spreading out the letter in God's presence had been part of the prayer. God answered Hezekiah's plea for deliverance, by sending a message of encouragement through the prophet Isaiah, 'I will defend this city and save it, for my sake and for the sake of David, my servant' (v. 34) and fulfilling that promise. After a devastating night Sennacherib withdrew (vv. 35–36). In his political crisis, Hezekiah shared the problem with God by physically spreading out the letter 'before the Lord'.

One way of praying for political and international situations, following Hezekiah's example, is by making a collage of newspaper cuttings and pictures, which are of particular concern, and spreading them out before God. You might prefer to assemble images on a computer. Another way of doing this would be to build a small cairn with stones or pebbles, with each stone symbolising a situation for which you are praying. Whichever way you use, you pray by laying the problems out in God's presence.

Praying our emotions

Creative/intercession

Jeremiah has listened to God and obeyed by publicly standing in the temple courtyard to declare to all the people that disaster will fall on the city of Jerusalem and the surrounding villages because of their disobedience. As a result, the chief officer in the temple, with responsibility for punishing troublemakers, has had Jeremiah beaten and put into the stocks overnight. This prayer of absolute honesty follows on from this punishment.

Read Jeremiah 20:7–18.

Notice the mood swings as Jeremiah prays.

In verses 7–10 he pours out his feelings about God to God. He feels deceived by God and tells him so. There is no diplomatic language here. In spite of obeying God, he is persecuted and mocked. Even his friends want to harm him. However, God's word is 'in my heart like a fire' (v. 9) and he cannot contain it. Jeremiah is churned up and full of misery.

Next he turns to God for justice (vv. 11–12). It is almost as if he is pleading, 'Look, God, I am your servant. This should not happen. Sort it out for me!' Then in verse 13 he turns to praising God, who has a proven record of rescue. But in verses 14–18 Jeremiah is in deep despair again. He wishes that he had never been born and tells God exactly how he is feeling in no uncertain terms. The prayer ends on this low but honest note.

Praying with absolute honesty can be difficult. We can think that we ought to pray politely or in a certain pattern and that it is not right to talk to God in such a forthright way. Sometimes we have to recognise or acknowledge our true feelings to ourselves first. Also, we might know that God is aware of how we are feeling, but something might hold us back from telling him.

How are you feeling at this moment? Whether it is joy,

boredom, fear or despair, or something else, maybe a mixture of emotions, try to be absolutely honest with God.

Sit with a black or grey piece of cloth or paper in front of you. Place a cross on it. Now pray for all those in despair or feeling misunderstood. As you pray for those with other emotions, place different strips of coloured paper or cloth around your cross. Where are you in all this?

Looking back

Creative

As you look back over this section using some of the prayers in the Old Testament, return to the promise in the opening section where God is saying, 'When you (*your name*) call upon me and come and pray to me, I will hear you. When you (*your name*) search for me, you will find me; if you (*your name*) seek me with all your heart, I will let you find me' (Jeremiah 29:12, NRSV).

Fold a piece of paper in half. Then open it out so that you have two columns.

First look towards God. What is there about the nature of God that you have noticed through using these prayers? Write them on the left of the paper.

Now consider the people of the Old Testament who prayed these prayers. Are there any ways in which these characters prayed that have felt particularly meaningful for you? Write them on the right-hand side of the paper.

How will you respond to these insights through prayer or action?

Turn the paper over and on the other side write a prayer of thanks or a promise of action to the God whom you have seen in these Old Testament prayers and who is still our God today.

Themes from Ephesians

Pamela Evans

Paul's letter to the Ephesians

Introduction

How do you visualise Paul's demeanour while dictating his letters? In my mind's eye, I see him striding about, waving his arms to add emphasis, pausing occasionally to allow his scribe to catch up. In this section we'll be dipping into the letter he wrote to Ephesus, a strategic centre on major trade routes in the area we now know as Turkey. The local Christians knew Paul well, and there was considerable mutual affection (see, for example, Acts 20:17–38). It's suggested that the letter was also to be passed to churches that he'd been unable to visit, or where he'd spent little time. That would explain why it covers many of the basics of doctrine and discipleship.

As a focal point for reflection, I'd like to suggest this verse: 'It's in Christ that we find out who we are and what we are living for' (Ephesians 1:11, *THE MESSAGE*). Write 'Who we are' and 'What we are living for' at the top of a sheet of paper. Quickly (taking *no more than three minutes*) list under each heading the first five things that come to mind. Tuck the paper in your Bible, and return to it when you feel prompted to add something. You might find it interesting or useful to repeat the three-minute exercise at the end of this section.

As we work with Ephesians, look for times when you can read Paul's letter aloud, allowing your voice to respond to the text and your heart to be stirred as you listen. Try to imagine how the first recipients might have felt as they heard it read, knowing that their friend and brother was writing from prison—and that challenges were also heading their way.

In Christ, our inheritance guaranteed

Creative

Take three strips of fabric of similar length, preferably different in colour, to represent Father, Son and Holy Spirit. If you have a variety of colours available, take a moment to consider which might be most appropriate. The strips need to be wide enough to be rolled up and to stay rolled. (If you have no spare fabric, you could use household cloths, or even single bed sheets for an up-sized version!) You will also need a shorter, thinner strip of fabric or paper to represent those of us who have been 'included in Christ' (1:13, NIV).

Take the three strips and roll each of them into a thinner strand. Knot them together at one end to portray the oneness of the triune God. Plait the three strands together for about one third of their length, symbolising their relationship. Then place the thinner strip, so that it is completely hidden inside the rolled strip chosen to symbolise Jesus, and plait the three large strips a little further. We who have been included in Christ are now not only held securely 'in him' but are also encompassed by the strand representing the Holy Spirit and held close to the strand representing the Father.

Use the plait as a starting point for a conversation with God about what it means for us to be 'in Christ', with the Holy Spirit guaranteeing our inheritance (vv. 14, 18; also Colossians 1:12–14). Are there things for which you'd like to thank him, or questions you'd like to ask him? The Holy Spirit is also referred to as a seal, a mark of authority or authenticity and a sign of legal ownership (see v. 14). Allow God to speak to you about what it means for you to have been authenticated as 'one of his'.

Prayer focus

Thanksgiving and intercession

Ask God to bring to mind those brothers and sisters in Christ for whom he'd like you to pray today. You may already have pictures of them in your prayer diary or displayed nearby. If not, write each person's name on a slip of paper. (If you'd like to start using photos as prompts to prayer, you could search for them later.)

'I have not stopped giving thanks for you' (Ephesians 1:16).

Lay the first photo or slip of paper before God. Thank him for that person's faith in Christ and the love they have shown for his people (v. 15). Allow the Holy Spirit to bring to mind other attributes, for example, the strength of character that equips them to live to his glory in difficult circumstances; their wisdom or their kindness. Continue to thank God for them. If more difficult aspects come to mind, don't let these draw the focus away from thanksgiving. I have no doubt that Paul's fellow Christians were a mixed bunch but, on this occasion at least, he thanked God for them without reservation!

Take the other photos or slips one by one and do the same. As you go through, ask God to show you if it would be appropriate to write a card or email to one of these individuals, saying something like, 'You came to mind today, and I thanked God for you.'

If thankfulness seems to be taking up all the time available, there's no need to hurry.

'I keep asking' (1:17).

Invite the Holy Spirit to lead you as you pray Ephesians 1:17–19a for each of the people for whom you thanked God just now. Does God want you to concentrate on one particular request, or to spend most of the time interceding for one person? For whom does he want you to 'keep asking' in the days ahead?

The Head, far above all

Creative

Close your eyes and allow the words 'The Head' to flash images on to the cinema screen of your mind. What do you see? For many of us, they are inextricably linked with schooldays and the nervous chill that descended, even in high summer, while waiting outside the head teacher's door. For others, similar-sounding titles such as 'The Boss' may elicit memories ranging from a helpful, nurturing ward sister to an unapproachable head of department or a driven head coach shouting at everyone to *try harder*! Can you put a name to the feelings that are evoked in *you*? (If any is particularly troublesome, take time to take it to God.)

Coming back to the present, bring to mind those who are in authority over you now. Take a large sheet of paper and, in the bottom half of it, sketch (or diagram) yourself in relation to these people and institutions. Then read Ephesians 1:19b–23. In the top half of the sheet, by means of symbols (for example, a throne) represent the risen Christ's position at the right hand of God, and his overarching authority that extends to the community in which you live, work and serve.

'All governments are under God' (Romans 13:1, THE MESSAGE). Paul urges us to pray for *all* who exercise authority (1 Timothy 2:1–4), not just those who obey and honour God. It's good to develop the habit of praying from the perspective the verses from Ephesians can bring. Start by focusing on Christ, seated in the ultimate position of authority. Then use your sketch to guide your prayers. Are there particular officials for whom you struggle to pray? If you have been wounded by the ungodly exercise of authority, why not bring these wounds to God, for healing? Is there anyone he might be asking you to be willing to forgive?

Needing a rescuer?

Creative

> Trapped in the mire… sinking… sunk.
> So like a freeway, that road to the swamp—
> A highway to somewhere I might want to go
> But it isn't. I know, now I'm stuck.

Have you ever felt stuck? Mired up to your neck, somewhere you didn't want to be? Perhaps you know how you ended up there although maybe, even with 20/20 hindsight, you still can't spot where you went wrong. If you have clay or other modelling material to hand, talk to God about your experience while creating a piece entitled 'Stuck'.

If you've ever disobeyed a specific warning from God, you'll know the feelings of despair that flow in when problems arise: 'It's all my fault. How on earth am I going to get myself out of this mess…?' (See Luke 15:18; the prodigal son made one good decision!) When we're far from God (Ephesians 2:1–3), we may doubt his love for us and fear the consequences of throwing ourselves on his mercy. Oswald Chambers offers wise advice: 'Believe God is always the God you know him to be when you are nearest to him' (*My Utmost for His Highest*, special updated edition, ed. James Reimann, Discovery House, 1995, 2 January). How would you describe 'the God you know him to be when you are nearest to him'? Read Ephesians 2:4–10, making a note of what these verses reveal about God and his plans for us. When you've finished, turn the notes into a prayer of thanksgiving: 'Thank you, Father, that you are... And thank you that your plans include...' You could write your own poem about your experience of being rescued by God.

Built together for a purpose

Going out

If you have access to a building that has been constructed using stones of different shapes and sizes, arrange to visit it, taking a soft graphite pencil or a wax crayon and some large pieces of paper. (Alternatively, look for images of historic buildings on the internet or in a book, and engage your imagination.) If you are able to touch the walls, trace around the stones with your fingers. Feel the irregularities on their surfaces. Do some look very rough and ready? How well do the individual stones sit together? Is there a large cornerstone giving alignment and stability to the whole wall? If possible, and taking care not to mark the stonework, place a sheet of paper on the wall and gently rub the pencil or crayon over it so that the wall's features appear on the paper. You could also photograph the wall.

Marvel at craftsmen who, in years gone by, laboured by hand to shape stones until they were fit for making beautiful buildings. Over time, Father God lovingly shapes us, too. We may find this uncomfortable, but it's done with a purpose: that we may become 'a holy temple built by God, all of us built into it, a temple in which God is quite at home' (2:21–22, *THE MESSAGE*). Are you aware of having been shaped by him? Have you found greater stability as you have settled into 'alignment' with Christ? Thank God for his faithful shaping, and for including you in his dwelling place. Bring him any concerns, fears or questions that arise.

Us and them?

Bible study

The status quo was that Gentiles were outsiders, 'excluded from citizenship in Israel and foreigners to the covenants of the promise, without hope and without God in the world' (2:12, NIV).

Write the text of Ephesians 3:6 on a piece of paper, and roll it up like a scroll. Stand up, walk forward, and read from your scroll in the manner of someone making an internationally important declaration. Imagine the shocked silence, followed by a tremendous hubbub. Can anyone believe it? God's plan had been to bless other nations through the Jews (Isaiah 49:6), but surely Gentiles would still be outsiders? In the years since Jesus' crucifixion this issue had caused controversy (see, for example, Galatians 2). Is this really the last word on the matter? Paul's letter was sent to an area in which most people were Gentiles. Put yourself in the place of one of them and read Ephesians 2:17–22. Can you believe the good news in these words?

Turning to the present day, visualise your church community gathered for worship and thank God for everyone who comes to mind. If you're an established member, it may be difficult to judge how welcoming your church feels to newcomers. Those experiencing rejection in other settings on account of their ethnicity or social group may linger on the margins, wondering if it really is possible to belong.

Who are the 'outsiders' in your neighbourhood? How do you identify them, by their clothes, or by behaviour that seems strange or even offensive to you? Do you know any of them personally? We know that all men and women have been made in the image of God (Genesis 1:26), and that Father God 'has compassion on all he has made' (Psalm 145:9), so there's always some common ground. Take time to be still before God. Ask him to guide you as you reflect on the scriptures you have read, the thoughts and feelings they have evoked, and your response.

Together, rooted in God's love

Going out/creative

If you are able, take a Bible to a park or a rural area and stand in the middle of an open space. (Alternatively, bring to mind an area that you know well.) Turn round very slowly, looking to the limits of your vision at every point. Do you know what lies beyond? Now look up. How far can you see? Move to an area of woodland. Stand among the trees and look at the roots that go deep into the soil. They are drawing strength from its nutrients, and refreshment from moisture that's there even if it's not currently visible. The views you saw before are now hidden. God's power and love have no limits, but our awareness of them varies.

Standing amidst the trees, read Paul's prayer (Ephesians 3:14–21). Bring to mind one or two people who may be finding it difficult to comprehend the extent of God's love. As you sense the solid ground supporting your feet, ask God to draw their roots more deeply into him. Pray that he will enlarge their vision of his love for them and remove any blockages. Take a photo of the trees to encourage continuing prayer, or pick up another memento of your time such as a dry twig, a symbol of being in need of refreshment.

Back home, take a large piece of paper. Using coloured pens, write out verses 20 and 21, emphasising some words (for example 'immeasurably' and 'glory') by using larger letters and brighter colours. If you wish, you could also incorporate thoughts from the earlier verses, and add pictures. If using this reflection in a group, why not ask each member to write a few of the words, and to share any mementos collected? As the body of Christ *together* we see more of God's love, more answered prayer and more of his glory than we could ever apprehend as individuals.

All different, serving God together

Intercession

Some brothers and sisters in Christ really struggle with 'togetherness': they just want to get the job done, whatever the job may be, without all the chatting. Others find their more focused friends hard to deal with: for them, 'church' is meaningful relationships, not tasks waiting to be done. Both groups may sigh, 'Why can't the others be more like us?' Sound familiar? Where do you think you lie on the continuum between togetherness and tasking? Imagine what might happen if we all insisted on joining churches full of people exactly like us!

In 1 Corinthians 12, 'Paul juxtaposes the teaching on diverse spiritual gifts and the individuality of the parts of the body in order that the ideas might complement and give weight to one another. Diversity is an intended feature of normal body life... Some find it threatening, and on occasions the Enemy uses this as a lever to promote division. But the diversity is God-given, and given for our good... We opt for uniformity at our peril!' (Pamela Evans, *Building the Body*, BRF, 2002, p. 17).

Take a moment to bring to God any concerns or questions. Then, to overcome any fog brought by familiarity, read some verses in this modern version:

*Christ handed out gifts of apostle, prophet, evangelist,
and pastor-teacher to train Christians in skilled
servant work, working within Christ's body, the
church, until we're all moving rhythmically and easily
with each other, efficient and graceful in response to
God's Son, fully mature adults, fully developed within
and without, fully alive like Christ.... God wants us to
grow up, to know the whole truth and tell it in love—
like Christ in everything. We take our lead from Christ,
who is the source of everything we do. He keeps us in
step with each other. His very breath and blood flow
through us, nourishing us so that we will grow up
healthy in God, robust in love.*

EPHESIANS 4:11–13, 15–16, *The Message*

The gifts the Spirit brings are not rewards or long-service
medals; they're 'grace gifts', freely and generously given
as God pleases, so that all may move towards maturity and
be equipped to serve him in diverse ways (see also Romans
12:4–8). Reread the verses from Ephesians, turning them into
a prayer for your church. For example, 'Father, thank you for
the gifts we have received as a church family... help us to work
together as one. Jesus, we need you to keep us in step. May
we draw nourishment from you and grow to be a healthy, fully
alive, Christ-like community'.

Children of the light

Creative

I don't have to DIY a 'new self' that's capable of living 'a life
of love' (Ephesians 5:2) and feeling at home in the light (v. 8).
What a relief! God's hand is already bringing this new creation

into being (4:24). It's like a garment received from someone who loves me, someone who knows me well, whose gifts I never want to hide in a drawer. Although noticeably different from my previous attire, it doesn't make me look strange, just... what's the right word? Lovelier, maybe?

Some well-worn jumpers and familiar outfits are difficult to throw away, even when they no longer fit the person I've become or only pass muster in dim lighting. A straight-talking friend can help, and that's what Paul is here: 'Get rid of it!' he says. 'And then take on an entirely new way of life—a God-fashioned life, a life renewed from the inside and working itself into your conduct as God accurately reproduces his character in you' (4:22–23, THE MESSAGE). My responsibility is to exercise my God-given freewill (5:11): to choose, moment by moment, not to entertain the old attitudes—the 'sad rags', fit only for life in the dark.

Read Ephesians 4:22–32. On some paper you don't want to keep, make a note of any specific sins or habits that the Holy Spirit seems to be highlighting. He points out such things for our good, so that they may be dealt with by confession and repentance; a vague sense of condemnation is unlikely to be from God. Then read these words written by another faithful friend: 'If we claim to be without sin, we deceive ourselves and the truth is not in us. If we confess our sins, he is faithful and just and will forgive us our sins and purify us from all unrighteousness' (1 John 1:8–9). In a fire grate, or a suitable place outdoors, set fire to the piece of paper to symbolise both purification and the coming of light into dark places.

(If you have found this reading disturbing, consider asking a trusted friend or church leader to pray with you as you seek forgiveness, release or healing from God.)

Love and submit

Visual

Reflections on submission may be hampered by interpretations imposed over the years, so why not begin by asking God to remove any accumulated debris?

For members of Christ's body, joined to the (one) head (Ephesians 4:4, 15–16), submission to one another 'out of reverence for Christ' is to be the norm (5:21). In Paul's first letter to the Corinthians, a long passage (12:12–31) on the theme of diversity within the body of Christ leads straight into teaching on *agape* love. Diversity brings both strengths and challenges, and the same can be said of mutual submission. Elsewhere, Paul had written, 'Be devoted to one another in love. Honour one another above yourselves' (Romans 12:10). Have you seen such heart-attitudes bringing blessing among God's people?

The Greek word translated 'head' (Ephesians 5:23; also 1:22; 4:15) can mean 'taking precedence over' but, as in English, there are other senses: it's also used for the head (source) of a river. That particular meaning sits well alongside thoughts of a husband being a source of blessing to his wife, loving and caring for her 'just as Christ does the church' (5:29).

Have you ever seen a tower of champagne glasses at a celebration? I'm visualising one overflowing with water, symbolising not only the life that flows from Christ but also the blessings church members and families, united in love, may share one with another. There are videos of towers on the internet, and you could invite God to speak to your heart while watching one. Towers include an element of hierarchy that you may find unhelpful, but they also illustrate the truth that the function of the whole body depends on each part (4:16) and the lower parts deserve special honour (1 Corinthians 12:23–24).

Refocus on the word 'submission'. Bring to God the thoughts and feelings evoked by the scriptures you have read and the images that have come to mind. If there is pain attached, bring this to Father God, and ask him to guide you as you seek release and healing.

Standing together

Imagination

Paul likened our equipment for the spiritual battle to the armour worn by Roman soldiers, a common sight in his day. He was writing to the church, not to an individual 'Christian soldier'; Paul wasn't exhorting anyone to stand alone against the foe. Read Ephesians 6:10–17 very slowly, visualising each item of equipment being issued not only to you but also to those with whom you worship regularly. Have you had the experience of benefiting, for example, from a word of truth spoken by another Christian? Have the shields (faith) of others enabled you to stand firm during a testing time?

The equipment described is primarily protective. The 'sword of the Spirit' is a possible exception, but notice how Jesus used words from scripture (Luke 4:4, 8, 12). I'm sure Paul was expecting church members to use scriptures and other authentic words from God to render ineffective the attacks of the Adversary, not to wage war against one other. Modern-day military experts have shown that 'unit cohesion' (found in a committed team with buddies who trust one another) reduces the probability of having to leave the front line because of combat stress, sometimes called battle fatigue. Given how often Paul wrote about unity in the body of Christ, I wonder if he'd come to the same conclusion!

The Romans had developed the *testudo* (tortoise) formation: soldiers standing together, shields aligned to form an effective barrier against arrows and other missiles (see internet images). Is this how it feels in your situation? Are there gaps between the shields? Are vital pieces of equipment missing or in need of repair? Move into a time of prayer for brothers and sisters in Christ and for your church community.

Reflecting on this issue

I wonder how you feel as you reach the end of an issue of *Quiet Spaces*. Is there a sadness that you'll no longer have the issue with that photo on the cover lying around, that there is an end to this part of a journey and the leaving behind of a now much loved travelling companion?

Or do you see the new issue when it arrives with its enticing neat pages and shiny new cover, and its new photo, and then become excited, rearing to start, to see what new gems there are inside and where you'll travel together?

Whichever way you view the end of an issue, and it may well be a mixture of both, it's a good time to pause and think about what has happened while you have been using this issue and to ask the question, where has God been?

If you have a prayer space you have been using regularly over these months, visit it and pause, or go to a quiet place that has been important to you and stop.

Acknowledge God's presence in that place and with you. Be aware of him sitting with you.

As you hold this issue of *Quiet Spaces* in your hand, notice what memories, experiences, thoughts, passages, and so on, come to you. Recognise them as a gift from God and thank him for his generosity.

Especially for this summer issue, as we head towards a new school year, even if you aren't governed by that calendar, there is a sense of starting a new season, heading into autumn, with winter beyond, and things starting up again after the lazy summer days. Where are you and where is God as you head into your autumn and winter life?

As a Child

Phil Steer

Receive

> *I tell you the truth, anyone who will not receive the kingdom of God like a little child will never enter it.*
>
> LUKE 18:17, NIV 1984, EMPHASIS MINE

As we have seen, acceptance of God and his kingdom is not so much concerned with intellectual assent, as with an instinctive and intuitive response to Jesus: it is less about the mind, and much more about the heart. For Jesus does not say here that we are to believe the kingdom; rather he says that we are to receive the kingdom. We are called not to believe a doctrine but to receive the free gift that God offers us in Jesus (Revelation 22:17). And we are to do so like little children, receiving God's kingdom just as a little child would receive any other gift: eagerly, excitedly, thankfully, joyfully. No concern about the motivation, no embarrassment about the generosity, no worries about what to give in return; just a simple, open-handed, open-hearted acceptance of the gift that is given.

But the need to receive the kingdom as a little child does not end with conversion and commitment. God's purpose is not that we receive a 'golden ticket' that grants us entry to the kingdom when Jesus comes again. The kingdom is not simply something that is to come but something that has come and continues to come, breaking into the world here and now. Yes, we receive the kingdom when we choose to follow Jesus, but we are to continue to receive the kingdom, day-by-day, moment-by-moment—receiving the opportunities that unfold before us, and the resources that God supplies, in order that we might live out the new life that he has given us.

I write this chapter with Christmas fast approaching. Children, of course, love Christmas. They count down the days, many marking their passing by opening the doors on an Advent calendar (and, increasingly, eating the chocolate they find within). There are just so many things for children to enjoy and get excited about: the tree, the decorations, the lights; Father Christmas and his reindeer; the exchange of cards with their friends; perhaps a nativity play at school and a pantomime at the theatre. Of course, top of the list for most is the anticipation of the gifts they'll be given on Christmas morning. Many, indeed, will have started making a present-list weeks, if not months before, itemising all the things that they hope to receive.

Young children rarely have any trouble filling their Christmas list with all manner of gift ideas (many of which their parents might consider of dubious quality and value). But as they get older, they tend to ask for fewer (if more expensive) items. As an adult in my 40s I am now at a point where I ask for very little, for there really is very little that I want—and when it comes to material possessions, this is probably no bad thing. I do wonder if this lack of desire has, perhaps, spilled over into the rest of my life—and, in particular, into my life of faith. I fear that I may have become too easily satisfied with what I have already received from God, and may have lost my heart-felt desire to receive more of him and his kingdom.

The Bible is full of warnings against the 'many foolish and harmful desires that plunge men into ruin and destruction' (1 Timothy 6:9). Desire in itself is not wrong; it is misplaced desire that is wrong. Perhaps some of us need to learn to desire again, to allow ourselves to desire again; to have that childlike longing to receive—not to receive the things of the world, but to receive the things of God.

The Psalms are full of such heart-felt desire: 'As the deer pants for streams of water, so my soul pants for you, O God' (Psalm 42:1). 'My soul thirsts for you, my body longs for you' (63:1). The prophet Isaiah declares, 'Your name and renown are the desire of our hearts' (Isaiah 26:8). The apostle Paul counselled the Corinthian church to 'eagerly desire spiritual gifts' (1 Corinthians 14:1).

Children expect to receive gifts from their parents at Christmas and on their birthdays. Such an attitude can, of course, lead to selfishness and ingratitude; but it can also be indicative of the depth of relationship between parent and child, that they know their parents want to give them good gifts. And in the same way, surely it is better to expect too much of God than to expect too little? For as Jesus said, 'If you, then, though you are evil, know how to give good gifts to your children, how much more will your Father in heaven give good gifts to those who ask him!' (Matthew 7:11).

But it is one thing to desire gifts; it's quite another to be ready to receive them. My young daughter does not have a large bedroom; in fact, she has to make do with the box room, one of the smallest rooms in the house. There is space for a bed, a wardrobe, a storage unit, and not much more. (She is looking forward to her eldest brother leaving home, in anticipation of being able to requisition his room!) This is somewhat unfortunate, as she quite possibly has more 'stuff' than either her parents or her brothers, with the consequence that her things have to be stored throughout the rest of the house. Even so, her bedroom still requires repeated clear-outs in order to keep it vaguely neat and tidy, and to ensure that there is some space available for all the new things that she receives.

For, of course, we cannot truly receive something if we have nowhere to put it; if our rooms—or our lives—are too full of other things. And while little children may need some parental encouragement to make room to receive physical possessions, we have much to learn from them when it comes to being ready to receive things that are of far greater value and importance.

Jesus promised his followers life in all its fullness (John 10:10). Yet we tend to be so full of ourselves and our thoughts and our desires that we have little room to receive the life that God has for us. Most little children are not like this. They are not preoccupied with themselves and caught up in themselves, not full of their own self-image and self-importance, not full of preconceptions and prejudices. They are not full of themselves and so they have room to receive: room to receive new experiences, room to receive new knowledge, room to receive new relationships, room to receive love and affection, room to receive all that life has to offer them.

We can know God's fullness only if we have this childlike capacity to receive. To be so empty of self that we have room to receive all the blessings that God has in store for us: room to receive God as our Father, room to receive Jesus as our saviour, room to receive the Holy Spirit as our guide and our counsellor, room to receive all the fullness of God and his kingdom.

And then, having received, we need to be willing to let go. We need to let go in order to pass on to others the blessings that we have ourselves received; and we need to let go in order that we might have room to receive the new blessings that God has in store for us.

Here again, we have much to learn from little children. Of course there are times when they manage to take hold of something that they want, and no amount of cajoling or coercion seems likely to remove it from them. In such circumstances perhaps the best way to prise whatever it is from the unwilling child is to give them something else. For little children are much less concerned than most adults about holding on to what they have, and much more interested in receiving whatever new thing is offered to them.

We adults hold what we have tightly, for fear that it might be taken from us; little children hold what they have lightly, ready to receive the new and greater gifts to come, the blessings that each new moment brings. And in their receiving, little children enable us to receive also. Just consider the pleasure that we find in watching a little child experience all that life has to offer, finding such excitement and joy and pleasure in the seemingly smallest of things: sights and sounds and smells and textures and tastes. As they receive, so we receive through them.

William Blake (1757–1827) encapsulates perfectly these two different ways of receiving—the adult and the child—in his short poem 'Eternity':

> He who bends to himself a joy
> Does the wingèd life destroy;
> But he who kisses the joy as it flies
> Lives in eternity's sunrise.

Forest Church

Bruce Stanley

I'll start with a bold claim which may seem obvious to many: it's that we're made (wired-up, evolved, created…) to function at our best when we're connected to nature; when we use nature connection as part of our physical lives; when we use nature connection as part of our mental and cognitive lives; when we're more practically connected to the source of our food, and when we worship God—who is in all things and is known through creation—while connected to nature.

I'm not alone. Many people can describe transcendent moments in nature where they felt deeply connected to something bigger than themselves. Forest Church is a way to explore that connection within community. Forest Church is a fresh expression of church, drawing on much older traditions when sacred places and practices existed outside, but it is also drawing on contemporary research that highlights the benefits of spending time with nature in wild places.

Forest Church started in May of 2012 and since then around 20 groups have started in the UK with more springing up in Europe, the US, Canada and Australia. Each group differs in its flavour depending on the skills and interests of those facilitating it. Some groups follow a structured, liturgical pattern around the changing seasons. Other groups differ what they do, sometimes walking and sometimes holding nature connection workshops into foraging or landscape reading. It is also a movement that is open and inviting to folk from other spiritual paths—meeting outside is neutral territory. Forest Church is easy to set up and practically free to run; all you need to gather are a few like-minded friends and, occasionally, a waterproof coat.

We meet outside, sometimes in the wilds, sometimes in a back garden or park to capture some of the magic and to connect with God's book of creation. This isn't normal church moved outside or a fellowship group doing an outside activity. We're attempting to participate with nature by understanding that it can connect us to God in unique ways and that God can speak through it. Read the psalms and you'll see that nature is already involved in an act of worship—we're remembering how to join in through our senses, imagination and our souls. This is great for well-being—getting out and about and letting nature's peace flow in along with God's—and it has an impact on how we end up treating nature. What you value you may end up taking more care of.

God is in nature as well as encompassing it (Jeremiah 23:24). Spectacular views or natural phenomena inspire spiritual thoughts and creativity but that's just the beginning. Connect to God through nature with all your senses—taste and see (Psalm 34:8), not just meditate. God is known through nature (Romans 1:20) and nature is part of the dialogue and worship (Deuteronomy 32:1–2; Psalm 19:1–4; 148:3–5; Isaiah 55:12) and part of Christ's redeeming work. If you're prepared to trust your instincts, a deeper reading is available, through natural theology which is the understanding of God, not through recourse to pre-existing scripture but by drawing on nature—a theology practised by Jesus.

Pioneering journalists like Richard Louv are doing a great job of collating the well-being and societal benefits through books like *The Nature Principle* (Algonquin Books, 2013), and organisations such as A Rocha are providing Christians with ecological campaigning.

It is vital that Christians engage deeply with nature and recognise our role as its advocate and carer. Gus Speth, a US government adviser and university professor, explains why. 'I used to think the top global environmental problems were biodiversity loss, ecosystem collapse and climate change. I thought with 30 years of good science we could address those problems but I was wrong. The top environmental problems are selfishness, greed and apathy—and to deal with these we need a spiritual and cultural transformation and we scientists don't know how to do that' (heard on BBC radio).

David Attenborough said, 'No one will protect what they don't care about; and no one will care about what they have never experienced' (Speech to Communicate conference, November 2010). So, can we start with the mission to re-enchant our view of nature? Get out in it and play as if you were a child. Forage and grow your food in it but above all connect and participate with it. Learn to read it as God's book as you would read scripture. Widen your understanding of how nature works and question the values behind how we treat it and stand up for it for the sake of your grandchildren's grandchildren.

Bruce Stanley lives in the Cambrian Mountains and produces wild and herbal teas for www.finepluck.co.uk. He is also a pioneer of www.forestchurch.co.uk and the author of *Forest Church: A Field Guide to Nature Connection for Groups and Individuals* (Mystic Christ Press, 2013). For further information on Forest Churches visit www.forestchurch.co.uk.

BRF Quiet Days

BRF Quiet Days are an ideal way of redressing the balance in our busy lives. Held in peaceful locations around the country, each one is led by an experienced speaker and gives the opportunity to reflect, be silent and pray, and through it all to draw closer to God.

Thursday 19 May: theme to be confirmed, led by Ray Simpson at Shepherd's Dene Retreat House, Riding Mill, Northumberland NE44 6AF

Thursday 9 June: 'Brambles and Blackberries' led by Bridget and Adrian Plass at Scargill House, Kettlewell, Nr Skipton, North Yorkshire BD23 5HU

Tuesday 19 July: 'Meet the Beloved Physician: A day with St Luke' led by David Winter at Douai Abbey, Upper Woolhampton, Reading, Berkshire RG7 5TQ

For further details and to book, please go to www.brfonline.org.uk/events-and-quiet-days or contact us at BRF, 15 The Chambers, Vineyard, Abingdon, Oxfordshire, OX14 3FE; tel: 01865 319700

Quiet Spaces Subscription

Please note one-year subscription prices below include postage and packing.

You can also purchase your subcription by Direct Debit. Complete the details on the direct debit form and post to BRF with the order form.

Please send *Quiet Spaces* beginning with the May 2016/September 2016/ January 2017 issue (delete as applicable).

PRICES FOR UK ADDRESSES

DESCRIPTION	PRICE	QUANTITY ORDERED	TOTAL
Individual 1-year subscription includes postage and packing	£16.35		
Group 1-year subscription postage and packing FREE	£13.05		
ORDER TOTAL			

PRICES FOR OVERSEAS ADDRESSES—INCLUDES POSTAGE & PACKING

DESCRIPTION	PRICE	QUANTITY ORDERED	TOTAL
Individual 1-year subscription Standard	£28.20		
Individual 1-year subscription Europe and economy	£24.90		
ORDER TOTAL			

Prices are correct at time of going to press and subject to change.
For information about group subscriptions, see overleaf or contact BRF at the address given on the next page.

Method of payment

❑ Cheque ❑ MasterCard ❑ Maestro ❑ Visa ❑ Postal Order

Card no. ⬛⬛⬛⬛ ⬛⬛⬛⬛ ⬛⬛⬛⬛ ⬛⬛⬛⬛ ⬛⬛⬛

Shaded boxes for Maestro use only

Valid from ⬛⬛ ⬛⬛   Expires ⬛⬛ ⬛⬛   Issue No. (Switch only) ⬛⬛⬛⬛

Security code* ⬛⬛⬛ (Last 3 digits on the reverse of the card *Essential in order to process your order*)   0000 **000** EXAMPLE

Signature .... Date ...... / ...... / ....

All subscription orders must be accompanied by the appropriate payment.
Please note: do not send payments for group orders. All group orders will be invoiced.

Name ....

Acc. No. ....

Address ....

....

.... Postcode ....

Telephone ....

Email ....

If you and a minimum of four friends subscribe to *Quiet Spaces* or BRF's other Bible reading notes (*New Daylight, Day by Day with God, Guidelines, The Upper Room*), you can form a group. What's so good about being in a group? You pay the price of the notes only—postage is free for delivery to a UK address. (All notes are sent to one address.) All group orders are invoiced. No advance payment is required. For more information, see www.biblereadingnotes.org.uk/group-subscriptions/ or contact the BRF office.

 BRF, 15 The Chambers, Vineyard, Abingdon OX14 3FE
Tel: 01865 319700   Fax: 01865 319701
www.brf.org.uk   email: enquiries@brf.org.uk
BRF is a Registered Charity (no: 233280)

The Bible Reading Fellowship

Instruction to your bank or building society to pay by Direct Debit

DIRECT Debit

Please fill in the whole form using a ballpoint pen and send to The Bible Reading Fellowship, 15 The Chambers, Vineyard, Abingdon OX14 3FE.

Service User Number: | 5 | 5 | 8 | 2 | 2 | 9 |

Name and full postal address of your bank or building society

To: The Manager ....

.... Bank/Building Society

Address ....

....

.... Postcode ....

Name(s) of account holder(s)

Branch sort code

☐☐ – ☐☐ – ☐☐

Bank/Building Society account no.

☐☐☐☐☐☐☐☐

Reference

☐☐☐☐☐☐☐

Instruction to your Bank/Building Society

Please pay The Bible Reading Fellowship Direct Debits from the account detailed in this instruction, subject to the safeguards assured by the Direct Debit Guarantee. I understand that this instruction may remain with The Bible Reading Fellowship and, if so, details will be passed electronically to my bank/building society.

Signature(s)

....

Date

Banks and Building Societies may not accept Direct Debit instructions for some types of account.